BAREFOOT OVER THE SERENGETI

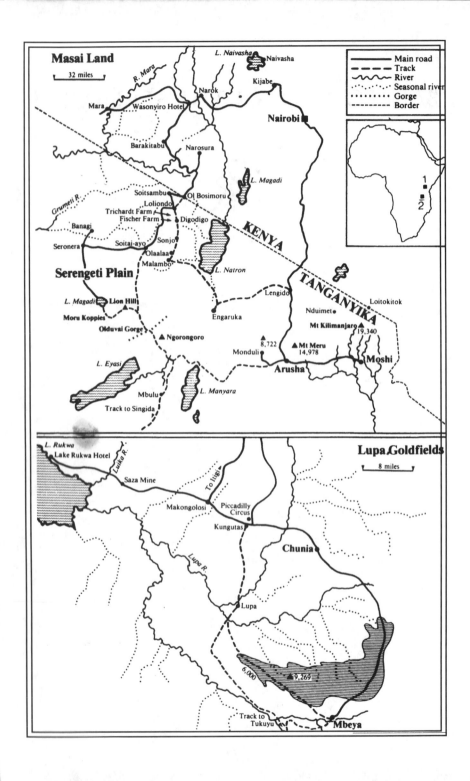

FOREWORD

by Steven James Jarrold-Foreman FRGS

"Barefoot over the Serengeti" is not some book title pulled out of thin air. It is a concise four-word summary of the childhood of the author, David Read.

Anyone meeting David Read today would find it difficult to believe that this was the same scruffy, dirty-faced kid who, much to the consternation of his mother, played barefoot with the Masai children that were his friends and constant companions at that time.

Tall, even with the slight stoop of age, with a demeanour that one might almost call aristocratic, David is quietly spoken and gracious, with a twinkling eye and ready smile that betrays a dry and somewhat wicked sense of humour.

Yet this polite and gentlemanly character has lead a life full of adventure and incident, which could almost be compared with that of Richard Burton (the English explorer, not the Welsh actor) or Wilfred Thesiger.

In the early 1920s, David's mother, having been abandoned by her husband, literally "set up shop" in the vastness of Loliondo; a huge tract of wilderness that borders the present-day Serengeti National Park in northern Tanzania. While the indomitable Mrs Read concentrated on building up a trading and hotel business for people in transit from Kenya to southern Tanganyika, young David made friends with the local Masai kids – one of those friendships lasting for over 70 years. His circle of friends included few Europeans at this time, and therefore David was more versed in the ways of the Masai than he was of his European peers.

Barefoot over the Serengeti, while recounting the adventures and tragedies that David experienced at that time, also gives an intimate insight into the lifestyle and customs of the Masai and their associated clans. David takes the reader on an incomparable journey though wild Masailand, as seen through the eyes of a child. It is a journey of discovery – not only of the natural wonders and wildlife that abound in this vast piece of African bush, but also of David's own self. The philosophies and lifestyle of the Masai opened David's eyes to another world, and it is this world that he shares with us now as we travel Barefoot over the Serengeti.

THE AUTHOR

ON HIS SEVENTH BIRTHDAY DAVID READ left the town of Kijabe to start a new and unusual life with his mother out in the great plains of East Africa, far away from the big cities and any semblance of European civilisation.

With only a few white adults for company young David naturally made friends with African children with whom he roamed through the bush and over the Serengeti plain, trapping birds, hunting for honey, chasing wild pigs. Scarcely able to read or write, by the time he was nine the boy was nevertheless perfectly capable of looking after himself alone in the African wilderness. The author writes of the alarming adventures he encountered as a child; of safaris over the great plains, and of the animals that inhabit them, describing the extraordinary and stirring sight of a mass migration: a vast tract of land transformed into a seething carpet of wildebeest, zebra and gazelles, lion, cheetahs and hyenas; of the migration he himself took part in - that of the fortune seekers who surged to the goldfields of the Lupa where they led a bizarre existence see-sawing between millionairedom and utter poverty.

Most of all, however, this book is about David Read's friendship with the Masai people and about the customs and life-style of this highly individual nomadic tribe of cattle-rearing warriors. Being a young child he was easily assimilated into the African community and quickly became an accepted figure in the Masai settlements, speaking their language fluently and joining in the activities of the children. Sometimes inviting themselves to the warriors' meat-feasts the little boys would sit round the fire listening entranced to talk of fighting and hunting, and to ancient Masai legends-some of which the author here relates. Having thus come to know the Masai intimately, and having witnessed many of their strange rituals, David Read is able to describe in engrossing detail a number of the ceremonies - to us outlandish and even barbaric - that surround circumcision, marriage, the attainment of manhood, the initiation into elderhood.

A delightful account of a remarkable childhood spent in rural East Africa between the wars, 'Barefoot Over the Serengeti' also provides a fascinating insight into the life and customs of the Masai, sympathetically conveyed by one of the few white men who can honestly claim to understand this unique people.

Born and brought up in East Africa, David Read has spent most of his life there and has come to know that land intimately. A farmer, hunter, keen fisherman and boatbuilder, during the Second World War Mr. Read served in the RAF, the Kenya Regiment, and with the King's African Rifles. After the war he settled down to become a leading progressive farmer on the slopes of Mount Kilimanjaro in Masailand where his main interests lie, and where he spent the next twenty-five years.

David Read still lives in the heart of Masailand, at a small homestead on the slopes of Mount Meru in northern Tanzania.

BAREFOOT OVER THE SERENGETI

DAVID READ

David Read
Ngongu Engare
P.O. Box 423
Usa River
Tanzania - East Africa

Acknowledgments
I would like to express my thanks to the late Mrs E. Harvey, to Sue Pretzlik, Susan Wood, Erika Johnston, David Frost and Jack Block for their help and encouragement, and to Mary Minot for the illustrations. I would also like to thank my Masai friend Lollemben for his help in refreshing my memory on Masai customs and legends. A special mention goes to my daughter Penny who drew the original maps and to Pamela Chapman who caught the words as they tumbled out and put them into order, and without whose untiring interest and hard work this book would never have been written. Steve Foreman for redesigning and editing earlier versions of Barefoot. Nick & Catrin Parfitt for their help redesigning this edition and last but not least, Stephanie Harris for her selfless support over recent years.

First published by David William Lister Read in 1979.
2nd Edition by The Travel Book Club 1980.
Reprinted 1984.
This edition printed 2004.
Design and Layout by Catrin & Nick Parfitt / Catnip Design
P.O. Box 3070, Arusha, Tanzania.

ISBN 9987 – 8920 – 4 - 3

To Pat, my wife, for her patience and tolerance.

CONTENTS

LIST OF ILLUSTRATIONS

Between pages 123 and 134

(All illustrations are the author's copyright)

Frontcover photography by: Nick Parfitt

CHAPTER ONE

CROSSING THE SIABEI

*D*ONALD AND I LAY FLAT in a thick clump of Leleshwa bush and could just see the train coming round the corner before crossing the bridge and starting the long climb into Kijabe station. The other boys were still greasing the rails and our hearts beat faster as we held our breath and hoped they would be done before they were seen. The train blew its whistle and we saw them race away and dive behind some bushes to the right of us.

The old wood-burning engine was now at full speed, hurtling along in order to make the crest, but as it approached we could see the momentum drop away as the climb got steeper and the wheels began to slip.

'We've got it!' whispered Donald. And sure enough we saw the guard jump down on to the track and signal the driver to go back. The driver stuck his head out and yelled, 'Bloody kids again! Get some sand on the rails while I go back down the hill!'

The train went into reverse and the guard and fireman took shovels and dusted the rails with earth.

Time for us to leave and wriggle away to safety, the others smothering their laughter behind their hands. I tried to laugh too, but stopping trains was still a tremendous feat in my eyes and I remained awed. I was only six years and three hundred and sixty-four days old.

Donald, three years older than I, had helped me count the days to my birthday. He was the eldest son of Boyce Aggett, who owned the Kijabe Hotel where my mother had worked until three months before, when she had left me in the care of the Aggett family while

I

she built a small roadside hotel of her own at Wasonyiro. This was to serve travellers between Nairobi and the mining area of Lolgorien, and also hunting parties during the season.

Without my realising it at the time, my way of life was to undergo a considerable change. We white children had used a little KiSwahili when talking to the servants, but from my earliest days at Wasonyiro, English was to take second place, with KiSwahili becoming my usual medium of communication. There too I was to quickly learn to speak Kikuyu. My associations with other white children would, after a time, practically cease, and I would begin to speak and behave like a Masai.

Now Daniel, my mother's driver, had come to fetch me, and I was woken up early by the sound of the lorry in the yard. All the Aggetts were up to see me off and helped carry my little wooden box of which I was very proud. It contained all my belongings except for a bamboo fishing rod with a line, cork and hook, which Donald had made for me. I felt rather upset at leaving the Aggetts and my friends who were, until this time, all European children of about my age, but I was also excited about the journey and rejoining my mother. Added to this, it was my birthday and I had been promised a present on arrival at Wasonyiro.

As I climbed into the lorry, Boyce Aggett told Daniel to look after me.

'See that he behaves and make him stay in the cab between you and Wanjiro until the rain stops, and tell Niakiago that I shall go to Wasonyiro as soon as the weather improves.'

"Niakiago" was my mother's Kikuyu nickname and means 'the one who is always helpful'.

'You have no worries, Bwana,' Daniel said, 'I'll look after him and smack him hard if he doesn't behave.' He turned to me, 'Jump in there, my son.' He said, and told Wanjiro, his wife, to cover me with a blanket.

Sungura, his turnboy, was ready with the starting-handle. Daniel switched on and called out 'Pindua'! As soon as he heard this, Sungura gave three turns on the handle and the engine roared into life. He had to move fast as the lorry started forward almost before he had removed the crank.

We were on our way in my mother's Model 'T' Ford, on a trip of just over a hundred miles, which, at an average speed of twelve miles per hour, would take something near ten hours. This was considered to be very good going in those days. The year was 1929.

After travelling about three miles we moved into heavy rain that continued for ten minutes or so, during which time large sections of the road could not be seen due to the amount of water. In a very short while the sun was shining and we were on solid dry ground, travelling at a dangerous speed of nearly twenty miles per hour. I was itching to go and join Sungura in the back, but Daniel pointed to some corrugated iron buildings in the distance and said that, after we stopped there for tea, I could go in the back.

On arrival at the shops, a tall good-looking Somali came out to greet us and invited us into his shop for tea, but first we off-loaded Wanjiro's kit as she was going to stay with relatives for a few days while Daniel went on to Wasonyiro. I was introduced to Abdi the Somali, and his wife tried to persuade me to have tea, but I did not feel like tea so she brought some bananas and offered me one, which I ate. She then insisted that I take another to eat on the journey.

Meanwhile, Daniel was chewing doughnut after doughnut, washed down with gulps of tea. When he had finished, we piled into the lorry. Wanjiro patted me on the back and wished me goodbye, asking me to pass on her regards to Niakiago. I was told to sit at a place in the back between the bags of maize meal and general stores, which consisted of beads, eight-gauge steel wire, rolls of Amerikani cloth, and a bag of red ochre. When Sungura had completed his tasks, he jumped onto the moving lorry and sat down next to me.

Sungura was a young Nandi tribesman of about twenty-five, and to me a great hero; but to his fellow Africans he was just a good turnboy with a jovial nature who never took life very seriously. He was a fine storyteller; many of his tales containing only a slight degree of fact - the greater part of them being the result of his imagination.

He immediately set to, telling me of how the hyena was the most notorious of all Nandi witches. The hyena had been known to leave the Nandi forest in the evening and appear instantly in Nairobi in human form, always carrying a torch of bark and moss to light its way. Having done its tasks in Nairobi - invariably concerned with witchcraft - it would be back in the forest before dawn, once more in its animal form.

As Sungura finished this story, he turned to me suddenly and said, 'We are now going down the Siabei escarpment, where the turnboy was taken off the back of Bwana Findlay's lorry by a lion last week.'

I had already heard of this, as it had been the main topic of conversation among the kids at Kijabe for the last few days. I immediately went cold.

'What will we do if it is still here, Sungura?' I asked.

'We are going to keep out of the lion's way,' he answered, as he pulled the tarpaulin over us. I crouched underneath without saying a word and felt for Sungura's leg, which I held on to as tightly as I could.

4

The smell under the canvas, which had previously covered hides, was fairly rough, to say the least. I did not notice until some time later that the brave Sungura had not put his head under the tarpaulin.

'You'd better put your head under, Sungura,' I called, 'otherwise the lion will see you!'

But he replied that we could now come out of cover, as we had passed the place where the lion had been seen. 'Anyhow, I don't think he is about any more, as the game scouts have been after him and have probably already shot him.'

Suddenly the lorry came to a halt, but I was still in no frame of mind to show myself. I heard Daniel shout from the front seat, 'What's going on?'

Another voice replied, 'The bridge is down, but the European has arranged for those lorries on the other side of the river to take our loads on for us to Narok. We will return with theirs to Kijabe.'

'How are they getting the loads over?' Daniel asked.

'By ropes tied to trees.' Said the other man.

The lorry moved forward a couple of feet and Daniel jumped out.

'Sungura, keep an eye on the truck and the child. I'm going to find out what's going on.'

By this time Sungura had taken the tarpaulin off me and I could see three lorries on the far side of the river and one just in front of us. There were a lot of people talking and shouting above the sound of rushing water. Daniel returned with Jack Webb, whom I knew, who greeted me and said, 'I'm taking you and your mothers' stores on to Narok, but first of all we've got to get you over the river.'

I was no longer worried about the lion, as there were so many people about, and Mr Webb had a reputation as a lion killer.

'Where is your kit?' He asked me, and turned to Daniel, instructing him to take my stuff and the lorry-load of stores to the front.

On reaching the river I noticed a gap of about fifty feet where the approach to the bridge had been completely washed away. Two very thick ropes were strung from trees on either side of the river and a gunny- sack was tied to one of the ropes. This, I discovered, was for moving people across. The other rope had a tarpaulin folded into four and tied firmly at the top. This was to carry the heavier stores and larger people who could not fit into the sack.

The movement of goods and humans across the water carried on for some time, when suddenly there was a shout. 'Look out! There's a tree coming down the river.'

There was much shuffling and scurrying about and everyone moved back on both sides. Then I saw the tree, large and slow moving, its length sliding around and bridging the gap between the banks. It stuck there temporarily, rolled slightly, and continued its course. Work to shift the loads started again.

'They are calling you,' said Sungura, so I walked over to Daniel, who said, 'We are going over the river now, my child.'

I felt a sinking sensation in the pit of my stomach. 'What if the rope breaks?' I asked him.

'It won't, and in any case I'm going over with you.'

'But we can't both get in the gunny bag, Daniel.'

'We are not going in the sack,' he said. 'We are so big, we are going in the chenderua, which Bwana Webb has just checked.'

I followed Daniel and we climbed into the tarpaulin together. Ropes were strung through the eyes in the canvas and over the top of the larger rope. We were enclosed completely, except for a few gaps at the top through which we could see the sky. I felt myself being lifted off the ground as the men took the strain and the rope tightened. There were some slight jerks and lurches and we landed on the opposite bank where our cocoon was unwrapped and we clambered out.

'Now that was a very simple operation, my boy. When you get home tonight, you'll be able to tell your mother all about it. Meanwhile we must have something to eat and be on our way, as it's getting late,' and Mr Webb called to his wife to prepare our food.

Ada was a Kikuyu, and went everywhere with her husband. She was the only African woman I knew who always wore khaki trousers, buttoned down the sides. She wore them, she said, because she was on safari all the time and they were more suitable and convenient than skirts. Other African women did not like her, saying she was swollen-headed and a bitch, and not nice to know, but she was always very kind to me and, next to my mother, I thought her the nicest woman I knew. On this particular journey she gave me sweets and talked to me all the way.

Ada had prepared a lunch of bread, butter and a large tin of Uplands ham, which we all sat down to and enjoyed, Mr Webb adding big dollops of mustard to his ham. When we had eaten we climbed into his lorry, also a Ford, but much newer than ours, and set off for Wasonyiro.

CHAPTER TWO
INTO MASAILAND

ITH THE EXCEPTION OF THE SIABEI ESCARPMENT, the countryside from Kijabe to Narok consisted of small open plains interspersed with large areas of Leleshwa bush. This bush can grow to about ten feet but is usually no taller than a man. It is silvery white; its colour caused by a fine, white fluff which grows on the underside of the leaf and the young stem, but when the stem gets older the fluff falls off. Leleshwa has a very pleasant aroma when burnt, and the root is extremely hard so makes excellent charcoal. The young stems, easily hollowed out, are used by some tribes for making arrows, on account of their strength and lightness. Otherwise the plant is a pest, as it spreads and reduces good grazing land to useless bush. For those who might be caught short without the usual roll of toilet paper, the young Leleshwa leaves are very soft and have their uses.

The Siabei river and its approaches were covered with large acacia trees and the usual assortment of wild fig, olive and cedar trees. The country was rolling, but from certain viewpoints the very steep walls of the Rift Valley could be clearly seen. Game was abundant throughout, there being the usual East African plains animals such as wildebeest (or gnu), zebra, impala, Grant's and Thomson's gazelles, hartebeest, giraffe, ostrich, eland and dikdik, with the occasional warthog and lion. In the early morning and late evening hyena and jackal were also seen along the road. The whole of this area was in Masailand, but few Masai were to be seen except for the odd moran (warrior) herding cattle, and women and children at the occasional isolated manyatta (village). The average small manyatta is a group of about ten huts, while a large moran manyatta could contain anything up to two hundred and fifty huts, depending on the clan and size of the circumcision group (which will be explained later).

The Masai are Nilo-Hamitic, living off cattle, sheep and goats. They spend their entire lives moving from one manyatta to another, and a family may have as many as six manyattas which they may or may not occupy in any calendar year, depending on the grazing, water and disease situation in a particular area. These manyattas are normally situated in the high country where there is sweet grazing, but usually very little water. They are also found on the lower black cotton, soggier soils, either near waterholes or permanent water. The latter are normally occupied during the dry season when the grazing is fairly good and the ground is dry. The Masai also have what are known as their reserve manyattas, and these are on the higher, sour grass areas where there is normally water throughout the year, but the grazing is as a rule infested with tick-borne diseases; East Coast Fever predominating. These areas are only grazed in a very dry year when there is no other grazing, and invariably a number of cattle are lost from disease.

The huts, made and owned by the women, are each approximately twenty-five feet square. They are made of fine twigs, either Leleshwa, sage or similar, which are shaped into a dome-like structure about five feet high, and covered with a light layer of grass if it is available, or branches with leaves. The huts are then plastered with a one-inch layer of fresh cow dung, which is collected each morning; the plastering continuing until the hut is considered complete. The plaster is renewed every rainy season with a thin layer of dung to seal the cracks. A small hole, about five inches in diameter, is left on one side for the smoke from the cooking fire to escape. The door is made of wickerwork and is not attached to the building, being lifted into place.

The huts are built in a circle, roughly fifty feet apart, and if the owner keeps sheep or goats, a small bubble is built on the roof for the young lambs and kids. The circle is surrounded by thorn bush, usually leaving three or four gates, also of thorn bush, which are opened in the morning to allow the cattle out and closed again in the evening once the cattle are back inside. Once the gates are closed the manyatta is inaccessible from the outside and, unless there is very good reason, or prior arrangements have been made, the gates will not be opened until the following morning. Anyone wishing to relieve himself during the night does so in amongst the cattle and all the excreta is trampled in with the cattle manure.

The younger calves are placed in a divided section inside the hut for nightly protection. The hut has two beds; one of which is small, made of wood, covered with hides and completely enclosed with cow dung walls, leaving a little entrance for the occupant. This bed belongs to the woman of the house. Opposite and about five feet away is a large bed, up to ten feet wide, which is also covered with hides but only partly enclosed. This bedchamber is used by visitors other than the favoured guest, who will share the bed of the woman of the house. Only very small children sleep with their mothers; after the age of three or four, boys and girls move into separate 'dormitory' huts.

The average day in a manyatta is largely governed by the cattle. Just before first light the women collect their fresh-milk calabashes and hide ropes, dressing before leaving their huts if the weather is cold; if it is warm and dry they may or may not wrap a skirt around their waists. They go about ten paces in amongst the cattle and crouch down to relieve themselves, at the same time starting to sing to the cows, which walk up to the women to be milked. Some of the cows then have their hind legs tied together with the hide rope to stop them moving; however, for most this is not necessary. A woman will call out to a child to release from her hut a particular calf. She will then milk that calf's mother, allowing the calf to suckle one teat as she milks the others. Her calabash has a very small opening, about two inches across. Singing all the while, she will milk all her cows into these calabashes, each cow producing about a pint. When the singing stops, the elders emerge from their huts and open the gates of the manyatta and let the cattle out, checking by recognition that none are missing or sick (they do not physically count the beasts, yet they seldom make a mistake).

Once the cattle have left the manyatta, the younger children collect all the fresh dung for repairing the houses.

The women sort the milk into three lots: for drinking fresh, for mixing with blood, and for leaving to go sour. They sweep the living sections of their huts, every few days removing the mixture of children's and animal excreta from the calf enclosures. The women then light the fires and cook meat if there is any. Thin one-inch strips of olive wood are put in the fire, and when well alight are used to char the insides of the empty calabashes to freshen them (the milk put into these treated calabashes will keep fresh in these for up to three or four days).

These chores done, they move on to repair the huts, spreading fresh cow dung over the roofs and walls, filling in the cracks. A section is done each day. If the women have young children, they tend them in between their jobs, their daughters helping if old enough. On alternate days they collect firewood and water, which may be carried by donkeys, or by themselves if water and wood are close at hand. When the work is done they take up their sewing while the young girls go off to play with the morans. Should a married woman's lover turn up, she will feed him and probably have sex with him during this time. If the women wish to go shopping or have something to sell, this also is the time when they will do it.

When the cattle come in as evening falls, the women immediately start milking, the older daughters helping. If guests of the husband's age-group appear and claim the hospitality of the woman's hut, she will feed them and do any entertaining she may wish.

If the grazing is good and near home, the elders move out in the morning, after having eaten, and sit beside a fire while they watch the cattle graze, being herded by the bigger layonis (young boys) and employed or poor elders. If the grazing is poor and a long way off, some of the morans will go with the cattle, moving at a fair pace, as they might have to travel as far as six miles or more for good grass and water. In this case, the elders may go visiting other manyattas or remain sitting under their tree, calling their women to bring food when they are hungry. Should there be a brew of beer in the manyatta, they will congregate there and slowly get sloshed, all the while boasting about their cattle and telling stories they have told a thousand times before.

On very hot days, the elders may stay under a tree all day, talking and sleeping until the cattle come home. Once again, having received reports from the herders, they will check the cattle carefully before closing the gates, choose the hut they wish to spend the night in, have something to eat, and then retire for the night.

The herders will water the cattle at midday and graze them home so as to arrive just before dark (in East Africa the sun sets all the year round between half past six and seven). On returning to the manyatta, they hand over any newborn calves to the women, have something to eat and go off to their respective sleeping quarters.

The morans who have not gone out with the cattle will either spend the day playing with the nditos (young girls) who are not busy, or going out hunting or visiting other manyattas and nditos. They may, too, go to an olpul (feast) of their own, or call in at neighbouring olpuls for the day, all the while planning some raid or lion-hunting trip or something that will better their reputations.

In the meantime, after the cattle have left in the morning, the younger members of the manyatta - layonis and the older nditos - take out the calves and remain with them all day. They stay close to the manyatta, so that they can be called upon to do any additional jobs if necessary during the course of the day.

This was the sort of activity that was going on around us, at that time largely unknown and unseen by me, as we travelled through Masailand en route to Wasonyiro.

We reached Narok just as it was getting dark and the news was that the ten-mile road ahead to Wasonyiro was very wet and sticky. Before going on we stopped at Mr Singh's store where we had a curry supper. Jack Webb had several drinks for the road, but at last we got away and reached Wasonyiro just after midnight. My mother was waiting up for us and I was given a hot bath in a little tin tub and pushed off to bed.

'Can't I see my present?' I asked.

'No,' my mother said, 'not until morning, as you are too tired.'

I was naturally very disappointed, as I had been looking forward all day to opening my parcel, but I knew it was no good arguing with her. I had not seen her for three months, a long time for a young child, and I felt shy and very small. She sensed this and quickly bent over to kiss me goodnight.

People say I inherited not only my placid easy-going nature, but also my size from my mother. I am not sure about myself, but she certainly had a wonderful temperament, with a ridiculous sense of humour; and she was most definitely tall - probably six feet - although slim in those days. She was dark and good-looking, with a dignified air when she was on her best behaviour, but very mischievous when she was not, both with her family and strangers.

An extraordinarily able and hardworking woman, my mother was quite adamant that she would not be an embarrassment or a bore to her family or anyone else, and was very determined to bear her own responsibilities. My father had come out with her to Kenya after the First World War with a bunch of other ex-army officers to grow flax in the Kericho area, but for various reasons the project collapsed. At about this time he was left a considerable fortune and, finding himself a girlfriend, disappeared overnight for an unknown destination, leaving my mother with a five-year-old son (my brother Norman), a three-month-old baby (me) and a large number of debts.

Friends rallied round and we were taken to Nairobi where we stayed until a job was found for her, managing the Tudor House Hotel in Mombasa. My grandparents on both sides wanted her to return to England, but as she had left home to marry a man much older than herself, against all advice, she was determined to stand on her own feet. However, when my brother Norman reached school age, he was dispatched to England where he remained with my mother's parents until he was seventeen. This was the only assistance she would accept from her family.

Tudor House was eventually sold and as my mother did not like the climate at the coast, she and I moved to Kijabe, where we lived until our move to Wasonyiro. Although not good, her financial circumstances had improved, and she had a number of friends who were prepared to help both physically and financially in the building of the new hotel.

I awoke very early next day and opened my parcel, which contained an airgun, two tins of pellets and two tins of Dairymaid sweetened condensed milk. This really thrilled me and was the nicest present I could remember ever having received. When my mother woke up she showed me how to use the airgun and gave me strict instructions that under no circumstances was I to point it at anybody - whether loaded or not - otherwise it would be taken away from me. Nor was I to fire at anything inside the hotel perimeter.

I dressed, was checked out by my mother, and went to inspect the hotel and grounds. The hotel consisted of one large main room, divided down the centre by a small three-foot wall. In one half there were a number of dining room tables and chairs and a large sideboard. From this end there was a door leading out to a pantry, and, adjoining this, a kitchen with two Dover stoves. The other end, which was the lounge, was furnished with wickerwork chairs with soft cushions and small wicker tables. The bar led off from a wide opening in one corner and behind this was a storeroom for bar supplies.

The inside of the main building was finished with split bamboo and the outside walls were plastered with mud. With the exception of the kitchen, all the roofs were thatched with grass and had no ceilings, so that looking up into the roof one could see the large supporting beams-and the spider webs. Occasionally a snake would be seen in the thatch and this invariably created a scene, as it would have to be destroyed. The floor was built up about eighteen inches from ground level with stamped gravel and was covered every now and again with a layer of fresh cow dung to harden the surface. Locally made palm-leaf mats were scattered about the floor.

The sleeping quarters consisted of six rondavels set slightly away from the main building. Each rondavel had an adjoining smaller room, containing a tin bath, washstand, jug and basin. Behind there were three long-drop pit latrines. All the buildings were whitewashed inside and out.

The servants' quarters and garage stood about a hundred yards away. This was where Daniel's lorry was housed and where repairs, both to the vehicle and to hotel equipment, were carried out. Daniel spent most of his time in the garage when he was not away driving, and my mother had put this particular area out of bounds for me, as she would not have me distracting him from his work, nor did she approve of me going to the servants' quarters.

Facing the north-west, one looked down the Wasonyiro valley for a distance of six or seven miles, while to the east, across the river, was thick Leleshwa bush. The vast expanse of the Loita Plains stretched away to the south-west and carried abundant game both in the dry and wet seasons. Often the game would come to within a few feet of the hotel buildings, and the only thing that would disturb them were our dogs, as my mother would not permit shooting either in the hotel grounds or nearby.

On this first morning I was introduced to my future stepfather who was at the time managing the Old East African Trading Company's store a mile away. His name was Otto Fischer and he was a Czechoslovakian chartered accountant on a three-year contract in Kenya. Apart from his store and the hotel, the only other buildings in Wasonyiro were on the far side of the river. These were three shops owned by a Muslim Indian, a Sikh and a Somali, all of whom were competing with one another and, because of this, constantly fighting. The only Europeans, other than travellers, were Mr Fischer and ourselves. During the dry season there were numerous visitors, some of whom were on hunting safaris and others travelling to the Lolgorien mines, but in the rains we saw very few white faces.

CHAPTER THREE

SIXPENCE FOR A BABOON

*T*HIS WAS A WONDERFUL TIME for me as I was allowed to do fairly well what I wished. Mr Fischer would occasionally take me fishing on the river and it was on one of these trips, while I was walking along the bank, that I noticed a branch of a tree move. Being a rather nervous child I shouted for Mr Fischer, who accused me of making a fuss about nothing and immediately plunged into a bush next to the tree. Suddenly I heard a scuffle and a rush through the undergrowth and then Mr Fischer was dragging me from the edge of the river bank. When he got his breath back he told me there was a huge snake in the tree and that I was to run to the hotel and tell my mother to send down as many people as possible with weapons. I was very excited and ran all the way.

My mother rounded up half a dozen of the hotel staff who, with their spears, bows and arrows, knobkerries and long sticks, followed me back to the river. On our arrival Mr Fischer showed them a section of a large python lying in the tree, which was surrounded by thick bush. This bush extended to the river's edge where there was a ford, the water being about eighteen inches deep over the crossing. A discussion started as to how the snake should be approached, but with all the noise and disturbance the python decided to make the first move and began to slither to another clump of bushes further down the river. Two men dashed round and cut off its retreat, so it turned and went towards the water. This was what everyone was hoping for. The next thing I knew Mr Fischer was telling the man with the bow not to use his arrows any more and the others not to spear it, as they would spoil the skin. During all this time there was a tremendous amount of shouting and dashing around. I took fright and ran across the river, about fifty feet wide at this point, to a bit of open ground.

But the snake had vanished. Everyone knew where it had entered the water but had lost sight of it. A young Masai boy next to me spotted it and shouted, 'It's here'!

He indicated a spot nearly forty feet upstream. He threw a stone, which hit the snake, but it kept moving. The cook, approaching the snake fast, went right up to it with his knobkerrie and a long stick, which he used to lift the snake's head out of the water. He swung at it with the knobkerrie a couple of times, and announced that it was dead.

The python was dragged out of the river by its tail, and I summoned up enough courage to go closer. Just then it moved and someone shouted, 'It's still alive!' Without any further ado the area was cleared except for the cook and Mr Fischer. One man in his haste sent me flying into the water, but had the goodness to turn and pull me out. I was screaming with both fright and pain, and Mr Fischer quickly came over to me and said, 'Don't be scared. It's only the snake's reflexes; the movement will go on for at least another half-hour.'

He then took me by the hand and led me to it, and allowed me to knock it on the head with a knobkerrie to satisfy myself that it was, indeed, dead.

There was great excitement among the staff. Everyone was talking at once; the only man who appeared calm was the cook, who stood aside in heroic silence. The snake was measured and found to be twenty-two feet long. There was a large lump in the centre of its stomach which, when it had been gutted, turned out to be a big hare, barely digested. The snakeskin was later cured and hung on the wall in the main room where it remained until the hotel was eventually sold. With the exception of a twenty-eight-foot python containing a whole Bushbuck, I have not seen a bigger snake to this day.

I was naturally very excited and wanted to know all about the python. I was told that it normally lies up along a game track, hidden in the bushes where it is excellently camouflaged, and waits for its prey. As soon as the animal is near enough it strikes, biting very deep into the flesh and then immediately winding itself around the victim and crushing it (a python bite is not poisonous, but if not treated the wound can go septic). The snake then covers the dead animal with slippery spittle and swallows it whole. If the prey is very large, such as a buck or wild pig, the snake will lie in the same place for a week or even more, digesting its food, during which time it is virtually incapable of defending itself.

After some time at Wasonyiro, we were joined by the Findlay family and their seven children. Mr Findlay had a transport business and based his two lorries at Wasonyiro. These were Fords of one-and-a-half tons each, driven by Mr Findlay and his driver. When he was old enough, his second eldest son, Dennis, took over and drove one of the lorries.

Dennis was a year older than I and even at that age knew quite a bit about mechanics. In later years, although he had very little education, he became one of the best-known motor mechanics in southern Kenya. When he was not playing about inside engines or driving, Dennis, his brother Gerry and sister Peggy and I would always be together.

A man called MacDonald turned up one day with a baby baboon

and a young puppy which he gave me. However, for some reason or other he insisted that it was bad luck to give away a monkey, so I paid him sixpence and named the monkey Sumuni, which is the Swahili slang for sixpence.

Sumuni grew up to be an unusual character. Outside my mother's rondavel was a large fever tree, in the fork of which we nailed an empty petrol box where Sumuni slept at night. After being with us for about three weeks the little baboon had grown considerably and became a nuisance to people staying at the hotel, so he had to be tied up. Unfortunately, he would get his rope wrapped round the branches of the tree, so Mr Fischer put up a pole with the petrol box on top and a metal ring around the pole to which was attached Sumuni's rope. In this way he did not get tangled up so often. He was also given a gunny bag with which he could cover himself at night, just like a human.

At about this time my mother, in partnership with Mr Fischer, started a creamery. The Masai women brought in milk to the creamery, where the cream was turned into clarified butter, or ghee, and the separated milk fed to the pigs, which were kept as part of the scheme. While the women waited for the milk to be weighed, Sumuni would sometimes escape from his rope and immediately run over to them. He would ease up and pretend to take bugs and fleas from their heads and, as soon as they were relaxed, grab their skirts and run. On two or three occasions he managed virtually to undress a woman. This raised a big laugh from the other women and the creamery staff, but no one lifted a finger to help the poor unclad woman. We found it great fun, encouraging Sumuni to do this by giving him sweets and condensed milk - which, like me, he was very fond of − each time he was successful.

One night, when we were in bed, we heard him cry out, but before my mother could reach him, Sumuni had been killed by wild dogs.

It was only a few nights after this that my mother, having worked late in the hotel, came into the room where I was sleeping and found a large black mamba curled up on the bottom of my bed. She was at first struck dumb and just stood and looked at it. When she came to her senses she put the torch she had been carrying down on the dressing-table facing the snake and slowly moved out of the room. A white hunter was staying at the hotel and she ran to his rondavel for help. Carrying his shot-gun, he and two of the servants entered our room. One of the Africans crept to the top of the bed and covered my head with the blankets, while the other knocked the snake to the floor with a long stick. The hunter shot the mamba and I awoke in a terrible fright and started screaming, not knowing what was happening. Had I known, I would probably have screamed all the more.

After quietening me down, the hunter told my mother that black mambas always lived in pairs, and that the mate would be around looking for the dead snake, so it was decided that we would move to another rondavel. Two days later the mate did appear and was seen by one of the servants following what we assumed to be the same route as the first snake. Mr Fischer shot it and we returned to our old room, but I never felt the same in that rondavel again and always looked carefully behind the cupboards and under the beds to see if there were any more snakes.

We had been at Wasonyiro a year or so when construction was started on what appeared to be, for that time and place, a very modern building. It was nearly fifty feet long by seventeen feet wide, and was divided into four rooms, two small and two large. It was built of corrugated iron with ceilings and inside walls of Kavirondo matting. I learned that this was to be our new house. The four rooms were a living-room, main bedroom for my mother and stepfather, a small room for me and a bathroom.

When the house was completed, my mother told me that she and Mr Fischer were going up to Nairobi to be married and would not be back for four or five days. When they returned Mr Fischer would be my stepfather and she would like me to call him Father. At first I felt a little embarrassed about this, but after a while it became quite natural and as we got on very well together. Anyhow, it did not really mean anything to me, whether he was my father or not. We remained good friends until he died and I knew no other father.

In conjunction with the hotel business, my parents kept a size-able herd of saddleback pigs. Part of their diet consisted of fresh meat fed to them twice a week from game shot on the plains. I usu-ally accompanied my stepfather on these shooting trips and once, just after the rains when the game was plentiful, my stepfather, two other men, Gerry and I went out in his boxbody Chevrolet.

A wildebeest was wounded after several shots, when it collapsed and was presumed dead. The car was driven up to it and my stepfa-ther jumped out, but at that precise moment the wildebeest got up and attacked him. He took cover behind the car but it began to move forwards, driven by one of the other men. The wildebeest, presumably seeing the movement of the vehicle, attacked it and ripped the tool-box off the side, getting its horn stuck in the alu-minium outer cover of the boxbody. My stepfather grabbed a rifle from the car and shot it through the head. It then took over half an hour of hacking and pulling to dislodge the horn from the metal of the vehicle. Since then I have had the greatest respect for these animals. Although they are supposed to be mild, I have on numerous occasions over the years been in situations where they showed a very fierce and belligerent streak.

This same day we shot four wildebeest, a zebra and a Thomson's gazelle, and loaded them on to the lorry, which had been following behind. On our way home at dusk we stopped to watch two herds of giraffe, which stood facing one another. From the centre of each herd a male moved forward, and the two then began to fight, winding their necks round each other; every now and then one would give a sharp tug towards itself and throw the other off balance. It would then turn very fast and kick out as hard as it could, making contact with a loud thundering sound. One giraffe would then walk off, pursued by the other, and the battle would continue. Eventually one was beaten and it loped away leaving the hero to be joined by all the females from both herds. The vanquished proceeded on its own until it was well out of sight. I saw these giraffe regularly for about a month after this, as they lived in the vicinity, and all the females and young remained with their new master throughout this time.

One day Jock MacDonald, who lived at Narosura near Barakitabu, stayed at the hotel. The next morning he told my mother that he was taking me on safari with him for two days. Mac, as everyone called him, had in the past been notorious for his poaching activities, but at this particular time was employed by the Game Department to suppress poaching.

We set off. After travelling for about an hour-and-a-half, one of his two servants suddenly pointed to lots of large birds two miles out on the right. We immediately turned off the road and bounced over the open country, which was dotted with acacia trees. We soon found the reason for the vultures presence.

By the side of a dry riverbed lay a dead wildebeest with only its tail cut off, the rest of its body intact. Mac swore and, talking to no one in particular, said he knew who the bastards were. In the next two hours we found a total of twenty-six dead wildebeest in the area, all with their tails cut off. It was obvious that the culprits were not African, as car-wheel tracks could be clearly seen; also, discarded "Passing Show" cigarette ends, and the fact that the animals had been shot with a rifle, all pointed to sophisticated poachers.

Mac told me it was criminal and wasteful for people to slaughter animals and not make use of any part other than the tail, which was probably sold to make fly-whisks. Among many of the tribes in East Africa it was a status symbol to possess a wildebeest-tail fly-whisk. Depending on the social position of the individual, the whisk could be fitted on to a handle of ordinary wood, or of ebony, or ebony with beads, or in the case of a very superior chief or witch-doctor - particularly among the Kikuyu, Masai and Kipsigis tribes - to an ivory handle. Also the hairs from the longer wildebeest tails were prized for the making of fine woven bangles, again to be worn by the upper hierarchy. There was, therefore, a fairly inexhaustible market for these tails.

On reaching Mara, we went to a small rest-house where we off-loaded the game and left behind the two servants. One was given instructions to go and collect the game scouts while the other man set up camp. Mac and I went to the river to fish, and that night we sat by a cheerful fire enjoying our afternoon's catch, while Mac told me stories of his shooting escapades on the Congo border. Arap

Koski, his turnboy-cum-driver, cook, mechanic and general facto-
tum, also sat by the fire after serving our supper and competed in
the story telling.

We slept in amongst the game, which let us know of their presence throughout the night. Hyena were attracted by the meat we
had brought into camp, and lion roared across the river from one
end to the other, followed by the yelping of jackal which were hoping to pick up bits the lion had left behind. I was beginning to get
quite used to animals in the daytime, but did not fancy the noises
they made at night. As a result I do not think I slept for one
minute, and kept waking Mac, who was competing solidly with the
lion. In fact I do not know which was the loudest: Mac's snoring or
the lions' roaring.

Next day we were up early, breakfasted on fish and chips, and
once again went along the river, this time with the car and the servants. After catching another six or seven fish we had tea at an
Indian shop and then carried on home to Wasonyiro.

CHAPTER FOUR

MY FRIEND WAWERU

URING OUR YEARS AT WASONYIRO, my mother tried hard to make a success of the hotel, and as a result did not have much time to spend on me. I was therefore allowed much more freedom than if our circumstances had been different. Looking back, I realise how difficult it must have been for her, especially before she remarried, and I appreciate and admire her all the more for this.

When the Findlays and their children, my playmates, left Wasonyiro shortly after my mother's marriage, I attached myself, somewhat naturally, to a Kikuyu boy named Waweru, who was three or four years older than I.

As I now spoke Kikuyu, there was no language problem and Waweru and I spent many hours together hunting for birds and rabbits along the river.

Waweru taught me how to make a bow and arrows and with these we became quite efficient hunters. We also met some other boys of about the same age, and once chased a Sykes monkey up a tree and tried with our bows and arrows to get it down. Unfortunately, an arrow struck one of the boys in the leg. Most of our arrows had only thorns at the tip, but this one had a metal head with barbs. The boy yelled with pain and we all got into a terrible panic, particularly so when, after the owner of the arrow disappeared, one of the others said that this boy had taken the head off one of his father's arrows, so it could quite well have had poison on it. Waweru was more under control than the rest of us and suggested that the only thing to do was to take the injured boy back to Niakiago (my mother) at once, as by this time he had lost quite a lot of blood and needed attention. In the panic, all the others, but for a Masai boy, had now fled.

On reaching the hotel I saw Jock MacDonald, who had just driven up, so I ran to him and explained what had happened. Mac bent over the boy who screamed as Mac quickly removed the arrow. It was all over so fast that I did not see how it had been done. Mac shouted to Sungura, who was walking down the road, and told him to take the boy to Niakiago for the wound to be dressed. In a week the boy had recovered and our fears of poison proved to be unfounded. I was very interested to know how Mac had removed the arrow, and he told me that any arrow with a barb had to be pushed through to the other side otherwise the muscle would be ripped away.

Mac, who had taken a liking to me, decided I was spending too much time roaming along the river and that it would do me a lot of good if I spent some time with him for a few days. However, as he obviously could not devote all his attention to me, I was allowed to take Waweru for company.

On this trip I learnt a great deal about Mac from his servants, most of whom had been with him for years. Apparently when he first came to the area from the Congo, he had taken up poaching for ivory on a fairly large scale, and at one stage, the then Chief Game Warden, incensed by this thorn in his side, decided to put an end to Mac's activities. Mac, meanwhile, got wind of this, so built himself a long-drop latrine with an extension underground on either side. The seat was in the middle with the secret trapdoors left and right. These appeared to be part of the floor, but directly underneath were large beams, and here he hung all his ivory. When the Game Department carried out a search while Mac was away, nothing was found, for nobody expected a man to keep his ivory down the loo.

In later years, the time when I knew him, Mac had a reputation as a very strict Game Warden and a severe critic of poachers. It is an accepted fact in East Africa now that ex-poachers make very good wardens.

I spent nine days with Mac on this safari, visiting most of his area, which was about sixty thousand square miles in size, running along the northern Tanganyika border. Every night, apart from two, we camped out, usually deep in areas heavily populated with game. Although Mac was getting on for fifty, he seemed to enjoy the company of children, and I thought he was a wonderful man, as he would always answer questions and explain exactly and carefully to me what he was doing. We found ten different types of traps for birds and animals, and Mac explained the workings of each one in detail, going so far as to help me make some bird traps when we got back to Wasonyiro.

When we arrived home I found my parents had left for Nairobi the day before, so Mac put me in the care of the servants and carried on to Narok. That afternoon we had very heavy rain and the Wasonyiro river overflowed during the night. The rain continued for three days, by which time the approaches to the bridge on either side had been washed away. The hotel was cut off and remained so for eight days. Food for the labour force was running very short, as my parents' trip to Nairobi had been primarily to replenish stocks. On the fifth day after the floods began, our head servant told me they would have to slaughter one of the trek oxen used for bringing water to the hotel, as everyone was out of food. This, I thought, was an extremely good idea. However, I did not appreciate the implications. The ox was killed and everyone seemed to be happy. But there were to be repercussions later.

The next day the rain began to ease up and my parents arrived on the other side of the river, but of course could not cross it as it was still in flood. In the morning the water had gone down sufficiently for work to start on the far side, but nothing could be done on our side for the first part of the day as there was an irate cobra in the buttresses of the bridge. At midday an old man chased everyone away and waited for the snake to come out of hiding. On its doing so he speared it in the back of the head and killed it. Work then commenced and by the next day people were able to walk across.

Although my mother and stepfather appreciated our situation regarding the slaughtered ox - the fact that it was one of the best trained trek leaders and that there were other, less valuable oxen which could have been killed instead, caused our headman to suffer a certain amount of abuse. He pointed out that he had consulted me, but this was not acceptable as I was only nine and not considered to be in any way responsible. It eventually turned out that the particular ox, a very fat one, had been on the headman's private list for slaughter for some time; and the incident cost him his job.

Shortly after the flood the rains stopped, without any further showers, which were normally expected. Now there was a shortage of food crops followed by a drought during which milk deliveries to our creamery from the Masai dropped. A number of pigs had meanwhile grown enormously in size and we had insufficient skim milk and other food for them, so their meat ration had to be increased. A lot of plains game had moved up river and we had to feed the pigs on wild pig meat, which unfortunately brought in swine fever to the herd. From five hundred pigs, the herd was reduced to fewer than two hundred in under six weeks. The surviving pigs were hurriedly put on the market and sold. We also closed down the creamery, as the return on butterfat alone was insufficient to justify its existence.

Soon after the closure of the creamery, while my stepfather, Otto, was up in Nairobi seeing his board of directors, the warehouses of the Old East African Trading Company caught fire and were burnt to the ground. Because of this disaster, the Wasonyiro branch was then closed down, and Otto found himself without a job. This situation required my parents to go off once again to Nairobi, presumably to make new plans. As they did not want to leave me alone, I was sent to Barakitabu, about twenty-five miles away in Masailand, to stay with the Webbs, who had, as well as their transport business, a shop there.

Once I accompanied Jack Webb on one of his transport journeys. We left Barakitabu at first light and after a while Mr. Webb pointed out a rhino, which was in front of us and slightly away from the road. As soon as it saw us it charged straight for the lorry. I was scared stiff and Ada, Jack's wife, screamed her head off. Mr Webb calmly continued to drive ahead. The rhino got to within ten feet of the lorry, stopped its charge, turned round and went off. We stopped and watched it disappear over the side of a ravine.

'Weren't you frightened of it?' Ada addressed her husband.

'No.' He answered.

'But why not? Rhino are known to charge cars and do terrible damage.'

Unruffled, Mr Webb pointed to a big run-off ditch on the right-hand side of the road, which, he pointed out, a rhino would not attempt to cross.

'How did you know that was there,' accused Ada.

'Well, I have been along this road at least a thousand times, so ought to remember something about it.'

No more was said.

We proceeded on our way to Ol Bosimoru where we were given

lunch by a Sikh woman. All the goods we had taken were unloaded, and the lorry was filled with hides. We left in mid-afternoon, the Indian having failed to persuade us to stay the night. At five we stopped beside a river and made camp; the turnboy went off to collect milk from a nearby manyatta and Mr Webb said he would start a fire while Ada and I went to bathe in the river.

Ada chose a secluded spot and proceeded to get undressed. She told me to do the same and jump in the river. This was the usual practise of the Webbs when on safari, and although Ada came from a tribe that in those days did not consider cleanliness - by our standards - to be of any importance, she herself was meticulously clean.

We had taken a four-gallon can to the river with us which we filled with water and Ada carried back to the camp. Mr Webb had the fire going and had put out three stones for cooking on. I went to fetch more wood and Ada boiled the milk the turnboy had brought. She was very fussy.

While she cooked our supper the two men tied a tattered tarpaulin to one side of the lorry and pegged the loose end to the ground, making a side tent. A groundsheet was laid under it as a bed for all three of us and I looked longingly at it for I was very tired. However, while the grown-ups had their usual drinks, Mr Webb and the turnboy discussed their experiences on safari, some of which were quite hair-raising to a boy of my age. These stories kept me fully awake until food was finally announced.

Ada turned out a first-class meal under rather difficult conditions. It was then that I learnt that she had previously worked in a European household, looking after the children, and had been taught to cook European food. It was also where she met Jack Webb.

The adults continued to talk for a while and then we all went to bed. I was woken up from time to time, by the turnboy creeping out from under the lorry where he slept to add wood to the fire, and also by the calls and noises of animals around the camp, some attracted by the smell of the hides on the lorry. In the morning, I asked the turnboy why he kept getting up to keep the fire going, as he was a long way from it and also it was quite a warm night, and he told me the fire kept the animals away.

After an early breakfast we returned to Barakitabu, and while I helped Mr Webb unload the lorry, Ada went down to her vegetable garden behind their shop. There she met some rather excited Masai morans who, when she asked what was wrong, began to abuse her, calling her a whore and a white man's mistress. Why was it, they said, that she spent her time sleeping with white men who were uncircumcised and dirty and not with morans. This made her very angry and she came rushing back, pursued by the five Masai, to report the incident to Jack Webb. One of the Webbs' servants saw this and immediately locked the doors and shouted to Jack, who got his shot-gun. He fired a shot into the air, which stopped the Masai. At the same time the Somalis from the shop next door appeared on the scene with another gun, all very vociferous and excited. Three of the morans ran off, but two were caught by the Webbs' servants and the Somalis.

It then transpired that the Masai, in very heated frames of mind, had earlier been over to the Somali shop, demanding pieces of cloth and red ochre on credit, which the owner refused to give them. One of the morans had then hit a Somali across the back with a stick, and it was when they were leaving the shop that they had seen Ada and decided to abuse her.

News travels fast in Masailand and within a very short time the chief and a local askarikanzu, who is a tribal policeman, together with a large number of elders, appeared, requesting Jack Webb and the Somalis to release the two morans, who would be dealt with by the elders. After considerable argument, none of which I understood, this was agreed to. The following day all five morans arrived with an ox and two sheep. This peace offering was shared out between the Webbs, their servants and the Somalis, and everyone was the best of friends.

This incident, however, did not end here, as one of the Somalis was later murdered. I remember overhearing Jack mention to Ada at the time, that if the Somalis did not stop messing the Masai about, sooner or later something big and unpleasant would happen. This was a feud of long standing between the Masai and the Somalis, and Ada just happened to be in the wrong place at the wrong time.

The Masai had little liking for other African tribes, whom they considered inferior, nor did they like the Asians. On the other hand, at that time, the Masai as a whole had great respect and liking for the white man. My parents, for instance - my mother in particular - were much respected and looked upon as rather superior laigwanans (leaders). For my part I think I can truthfully say that I was much liked and was spoken of with affection over a large area in central Masailand. In most cases the Masai looked upon me as a treasured son or brother of a somewhat fascinating kind. Most of the time I was treated with the respect given to a moran, while my attitude to them was that of a layoni. On three different occasions I was presented with a special ox of friendship by elder morans - a ceremony which is never extended to layonis – which gives the recipient the full and equal status of the donor. All uncircumcised children of the manyatta from where the ox was given would greet me by bowing their heads for me to place my hand upon, and the women would kiss me on the cheek.

Staying with the Webbs was always an enjoyable experience for me, as so much seemed to happen when in their company, but I was pleased to go home and be returned to my mother who had arrived back from Nairobi.

My stepfather had left for Loliondo in Tanganyika - and had, in fact, passed us on the road - where he was going to meet the District Officer to talk business. He returned two days later with the Sikh in whose shop the Webbs and I had lunched at Ol Bosimoru just a short while before. The Sikh was very badly wounded, having been shot three times between his knee and groin by a rifle. My stepfather picked up the Sikh the following morning and took him to the hospital at Narok. After being amputated, the leg was placed outside the operating room on the verandah for the bullets to be removed for identification purposes. Unfortunately for the police, a hyena appeared and the leg was never seen again.

Sadly, the Sikh died the following day. According to Sikh custom his body was cremated, but as there was no proper crematorium, wood was laid out three feet deep in the shape of a bed and the body laid on top. More wood was placed over it and ghee smeared on the wood. Then paraffin was poured on to the pyre and it was set alight. While the body burnt, the Sikh's wife made three attempts to jump into the fire but was held back. I did not see this myself, but learnt all about it from Sungura who always knew everything about what was going on, including what he thought was going on.

The full story then came out. The Sikh had been driving from Ol Bosimoru to Narok without any headlights. A European hunter came round the corner, saw the lorry and, assuming it to be a rhino, fired at it. It was not until he heard the passengers on the back screaming that he realised he was firing at a vehicle. He took fright, turned his car and disappeared.

At the inquest my stepfather was called in as a witness, but due to the fact that he was a Czech and could not speak very good English, he got somewhat mixed up with the questions. Having said that he did use that particular road frequently, he was asked whether he had seen any rhino spoor along the road. He answered, 'No.'

However, when asked whether rhino frequented this area, his reply was that he had seen 'rhino and rhino shit.' There was a hush through the court and the magistrate corrected him, 'You mean, rhino droppings.'

'No, your Honour,' said my stepfather, 'Rhino shit.'

The court proceeded as though nothing had happened, but for a long time he had his leg pulled about this episode.

The man responsible for the shooting, after thinking the matter over, reported to the authorities and was later found not guilty of murder.

CHAPTER FIVE

THE POPAT WEDDING

ONE EVENING MY MOTHER TURNED to my stepfather and said, 'Otto, what are we going to do about the Popat wedding? Are we going or not?'

'I think we should go otherwise we may upset them,' he replied, 'and in any case I should like to see a Hindu wedding. Also I hear that Mac and the Webbs are going too.'

'Well, we have to make a definite decision,' said my mother, 'as we should leave on Monday, and today is Friday. I'm told they have organised one of the shops for all the Europeans to stay in.'

Just then we heard footsteps outside and Jack Webb shouted, 'Anyone at home?'

'Come in!' called my mother, 'Where are you on your way to?'

'To see you,' said Jack. 'We got bored in the bush, what with all the rain, smell of hides and the flies, so decided to come into civilisation for a few days. Ada will be in as soon as she's sorted out her relatives who have been staying with us.'

My stepfather said, 'Go and get yourselves settled in, then come back here for a drink. There's no one staying in the hotel so you can take your pick of the rooms.'

After I had had my bath I went into the sitting-room to find that the Webbs had returned and were sitting round the fire. It was raining hard and the sound of this on the corrugated-iron roof and the large fire made the house seem very cosy and warm.

'You are staying tomorrow, Ada, aren't you?' my mother asked.

'I was going to ask you if I could stay for a couple of days while Jack goes to Nairobi.'

'Why, this is very unusual. Aren't you going with Jack?'

'I've decided,' Ada said, 'to let him off the leash. He can go and try some of the white girls for a change.'

My mother laughed. 'Aren't you worried?'

'Not in the least. Jack likes his women well tanned. He'll be back. Probably having learned one or two new tricks. No, Evelyn, I just cannot take these roads any longer. And the thought of going all the way to Mara next week is enough to put me in bed for days.'

'While on the subject of Mara,' my mother said, 'are you and Jack going to the wedding?'

'Yes, we are, and we hope you will go with us. Mac is joining us here on Sunday and we can all go together in his boxbody, which is far more comfortable than the lorries.'

'A good idea,' said my stepfather. 'We'd better take some hard liquor and tinned food with us as these people are vegetarians and I don't fancy four days on vegetables, sweets and lemonade.'

Jack said, 'Mac has already enquired about the food and it won't be necessary for us to take anything. I've been told there may be seven or eight Europeans there and special food is being laid on for the guests. After all, there'll be Sikhs as well. Just imagine them going to a do like this without booze and pork. They'd go mad in twenty-four hours!'

Although I had not been invited to the wedding, Ada soon persuaded my mother to let me go. Mother agreed on condition that I started to wear my shoes the next day, to "break them in" as she said. This was because I always went barefoot, not wanting to be different from my friends who had no shoes to wear. I became so used to it that after a while I hated wearing them.

Next morning I was up early and saw Jack before he left for

Nairobi. He told me he had left his .22 rifle with Ada and that she would give me some lessons with it. Ada was the only African woman I ever saw using a rifle or a gun of any sort, and she was a good teacher. We had two wonderful days, roaming the river banks, shooting and fishing and doing as we pleased.

Forty years later, Ada visited my mother who was then living in Arusha. She bore no resemblance to the Ada of the old days, and my secretary, who had just completed typing the chapter on Wasonyiro, could not believe that this was the same person. Here stood a very ordinary African woman, plump and middle-aged, in a long dress and with a cloth tied round her head. She was almost servile, all the old spirit seemed to have left her, and she spoke only in Swahili.

One can only imagine that life after Jack died became very difficult for Ada as she had grown accustomed to a European existence. She had one more liaison with a white man, and that for just a short period, during which time she bore him a son. This man then married a European and Ada was forced to return to her tribe where she lived with a number of different men, gradually losing her grip on civilisation and what little sophistication she had once possessed.

On Monday morning we set off in Mac's car with the lorry following, as it had been decided that it would be unwise to go in one vehicle. We were stuck in the mud on numerous occasions in the boxbody, but the old Model 'T' with its slow-running engine and high ground clearance managed to pull us out. I started off in the boxbody but after a short time the grown-ups' conversation bored me, so I joined my friend Sungura in the back of the lorry.

At this time of the year the plains were full of game and Daniel hinted to Mac that there was likely to be a shortage of food, particularly meat, at Mara, as none of the staff were invited guests. Mac very kindly condescended to shoot an eland for them, promising to do so as soon as he saw a good one.

We crossed a river, which was normally dry, sandy and waterless, but now, with the rains, it was flowing strongly. Along the banks grew scattered acacias. These in the dry season drew their water from underground sources. Following the boxbody up the slope out of the ford, we saw it veer off to the left towards a herd of eland. Daniel said, 'Your European friends must be mad, going after a herd away from the road when surely we'll see twenty herds of eland along the roadside.'

The boxbody went on for about six hundred yards, then stopped beside a tree, which was covered in vultures. On reaching it we saw why Mac had drawn off the road. A lion, three lionesses and two half-grown cubs were on an eland kill, and although the vehicles were within ten yards of them, none of the lions seemed in the least bit bothered about us.

The male had obviously had his share first and lay watching us while the others continued to eat, their muzzles bloody. Mac shouted that no one was to get off the lorry - quite unnecessarily, I thought. The lions looked far too big at close quarters. After a while the boxbody moved on and we followed in its tracks, stopping about a hundred yards further on where Mac and my stepfather got out with their rifles and aimed and shot at a large dark-grey eland. It fell and we climbed down to help load it on to the back of the lorry. Suddenly we saw the lionesses approaching and although

Mac tried to shoo them away they were determined to have our kill. We all backed away and jumped into the vehicles while one of the lionesses began to drag the eland off. Mac then said, 'Let them have it. We'll get another.' This pleased Daniel as he expected the lionesses to be on the lorry at any moment. They showed no fright as the motors were started, and we moved off to leave them to their feast.

A few miles on Mac shot the promised eland, which was a young heifer in good condition. The staff thought this was a godsend, for although they would have had more meat off the first animal, the quality of the meat would not have been as fine. Everyone was happy and cheerful and we arrived at Mara in time for tea.

This was obviously to be the wedding of the year, as the little town of only five small shops was covered with paper banners, and there must have been four or five hundred

people, half of whom were Asians, from all over the country. Most of the Asians we knew, but a lot we had never seen before. One of our Sikh friends met us and said he had been detailed to see to our comfort. He led us into the shop opposite the one where the wedding was to be held. The interior had been cleared out and new blankets, as was the Indian custom in East Africa, laid along all the benches and counters. These, and the big bed in the only bedroom, were to be our sleeping places. At the back of the shop was a small verandah with a long table covered with blankets where we were to have our meals.

The wedding festivities were to take place opposite in Mr Popat's shop, which consisted of a big front shop with adjoining bedrooms and kitchen, all enclosed by a five foot-high brick wall, part of which had been covered over with corrugated iron. It was in this courtyard-of-sorts that the wedding would take place.

After settling us in, Mr Singh informed us that his wife and her sister were to remain with us for the purpose of cooking and generally tending to our needs. He would have to go, he said, but if we wanted anything - anything but beef - his wife would arrange it.

Mr and Mrs Popat and the bridegroom's brother came to visit us later and told us that nothing very much would happen that day, but the following day the wedding would begin. We were the first arrivals among the European community, none of the others turning up until midday the next day, when the MacKenzies, their daughter Lucy (who was a little older than I) and two friends drove up. One was a man called Rowlands, whose wife had died the year before, and the other was an elderly man whom I did not know and who arrived drunk. He did not eat or sleep but did a lot of talking and drinking the two days he was with us. My mother thought he was extremely rude as he soaked himself in whisky the entire time and saw nothing whatsoever of the wedding.

The main celebrations began at noon when sweets and sugary cakes were handed round, followed by tea. The bride's uncle stood up and talked to the guests in Hindi, odd bits of which were translated for the benefit of the others. Then a procession of Indian women and girls walked through the village chanting songs. They were dressed in beautiful saris and wore red caste marks on their foreheads. They all came to our shop and shook hands with the female members of our party, the men having been told to keep out of the way.

Quiet reigned for a while, then just as it was getting dark the bridegroom rode up on a white horse. Lucy and I noticed that he was not really riding the horse, but was just sitting there being led, while his hundred or so male followers surrounded him. It later transpired that the earlier procession of women was the bridegroom's female contingent arriving and this was now the male equivalent. Hundreds of torch bulbs were lit and bangers were fired. The bridegroom stopped in front of the home of the bride and was led in on the horse.

He dismounted in the courtyard and sat down under a small canopy between two men in ceremonial dress. Chanting and speeches followed, then most of the guests departed and left only the close relatives and friends with the bridal party.

Back in our shop, Mrs Singh had prepared a wonderful meal. There was a meat curry made from goat, a lentil curry, big fat chapattis and steaming bowls of rice. The adults had by this time consumed quite a lot of liquor and were ready for their food. They had been told that the next day they must not drink at all if they wished to attend the wedding ceremonies, as the bride was to be introduced to the bridegroom and until this had been done there must be no smell of alcohol about.

The next day nothing very much happened until the evening, when the bride arrived in a closed litter from one of the other shops. She was surrounded by women and borne in her litter by four men who carried her to her father's shop. Inside the courtyard, the litter was put down in front of the seated bridegroom. Mr Popat rose, and after saying something in Hindi, walked over to the bridegroom and led him out from under the canopy and escorted him to the still completely closed litter. The young man spoke to the hidden girl and she replied in an undertone. He was then allowed to open the curtains of the litter and see his bride for the first time. He appeared to be quite satisfied as he grinned and spoke to her again. We children were then all ushered out.

We were allowed in again later that evening to be introduced to the bride and groom, and shook hands with them. The new husband was about twenty-five but the bride was not much older than me; I suppose she could have been about thirteen at the most.

On the next day, the last of the festivities, the bridegroom, accompanied by a number of young men, called on the guests to say his farewells, and was followed shortly afterwards by the bride who did the same. They were then bundled off in a car and that was the last we saw of them.

About a week after the Popat wedding, back at Wasonyiro, plans were being made for us to move. My stepfather was interested in starting a retail business for the Masai at Loliondo in Tanganyika, as he now had no job. Also, at about this time, the Kakamega gold mines, which supplied the hotel with most of its clientele, had petered out, so there was very little traffic outside the hunting season. Consequently the hotel was doing badly and, until it was sold, my stepfather's intention was to put someone in at Loliondo to get things going, after which we could all move down there. However, Jack Webb broached my mother on the question of his purchasing the hotel and a provisional deal was agreed. He would swap his brand-new two-ton Ford lorry for the hotel, excluding our house, which would be dismantled and taken with us. This meant that we would be going down to Loliondo more or less immediately.

The Webbs then had a further proposition to put forward. As the hunting season was about to begin they asked my mother to stay on at the hotel and help them for the first three months. They also arranged to hire the new lorry for this period in order to keep it busy. My mother and I moved back into our old rondavel and the house was taken down and reassembled at Loliondo by my stepfather, who also built a shop there.

While the house was being loaded on to the lorry in sections, a very old Kikuyu came running up to the gang of workmen, hit a young man on the head with his knobkerrie and cracked his skull. Then the old man ran off and was chased by a crowd of people. The victim was taken to Narok hospital where he died three days later. The old Kikuyu was handed over to the authorities, and we heard that three years before he had married the young man's sister. However, the bride-price was not paid in full so the brother began negotiations with a new prospective husband. This enraged the old man and provoked his violent attack. Sungura told me he went to gaol for two years, and lost his wife.

Although I was looking forward to the move to Loliondo as it was something new, I was very despondent about losing my friend Waweru, whose father had elected to stay on at the hotel. On numerous occasions Waweru and I discussed this and we decided to approach my parents and see if he could go with us. The answer we got was, 'We'll see when the time comes.' So we spent more and more of our days together. When we were not playing close to the hotel we would go to the manyatta to pick up our Masai friends and disappear, very often for the whole day.

CHAPTER SIX

I MEET MATANDA

*T*HE TIME HAD NOW COME for our move to Loliondo where my stepfather had rebuilt our house and got the shop going. The question of Waweru coming with us was again raised and there was a categorical 'No!' from both his parents and mine. There were many tears shed and promises made on both sides to run away from home and join up with each other. Because of my association with the native children and their obvious influence on me, my whole outlook was more in keeping with that of an African boy - particularly a Kikuyu at this stage - than with that of a European child of the same age.

The young African boy is much more disciplined in the customs of his people than would be a European child; on the other hand he has much more freedom. A Masai boy, for example, will never talk in the presence of elder males unless invited to do so. He will stop whatever he is doing to greet an elder male, and if told to do something he does not like doing he will nevertheless not hesitate if the order has come from an elder male (this does not always apply in the case of elder females). Among his own age-group, the Masai does as he pleases: he can swear, fight, practise and play sex games, and generally do whatever he wishes, and no disapproval will be shown - in fact he will be encouraged.

The boy will be used for any manual labour that may be required, and is never pampered. He therefore learns fast, and the competitive spirit is instilled at a very early age. A boy of nine will know what herbs are needed for the treatments of various cattle ailments and where to find them, and he becomes proficient in animal husbandry.

46

He knows what wood to use for roasting meat to bring out the best flavour, and which plants and berries are edible. He also knows how to approach dangerous animals and can use a spear to protect his herd against the smaller predators. Under African conditions he is much hardier and less prone to sickness than a European boy, and, in fact, is more mature.

So, although I was academically backward compared with white boys of the same age, I was far more advanced in the practical day-to-day business of keeping alive and getting about in the African countryside. Although only nine and a half, had I decided to run away from home I would probably have survived without any major difficulties. I could not write my name, but I could catch my dinner!

We now had two lorries, the old Ford driven by Daniel and the new one, which was driven either by my stepfather or my mother. The day we left Wasonyiro, the new lorry was loaded and my parents installed themselves in the locally made cab, with Karioki, Sungura and I perched on the back on top of all our possessions.

For the first leg to Barakitabu all went well and we stopped at the Somali shop for tea. The idea was to reach Loliondo that same day as it was only a hundred miles or so away. However, trouble started shortly after leaving Barakitabu. By six in the evening we were still twenty miles short of Ol Bosimoru, which in turn was a further twenty from Loliondo, when the lorry suddenly stopped. My stepfather shouted 'Fire!'

My mother tumbled out of the cab, and panic ensued. The bonnet was pulled off and everyone piled sand on to the engine as fast as they could, including me, who was knocked down, shouted at, told to keep out of the way and eventually hauled off by my mother. The fire was put out and a post mortem held. I can very clearly remember my mother saying to my stepfather, 'I don't know what you are going to do, and I don't particularly care, but David and I are staying here for the night.'

Karioki was told to take various things off the lorry.

My stepfather turned to her and said, 'I'm going to get this bitch to go, and we are going on to Loliondo tonight. If you don't come, you can fucking well stay!'

After a few more hard words it was obvious who had won. My stepfather buried his head in the engine and went on working, but Karioki and Sungura unpacked our requirements for the night. We had only two gallons of water left and it tasted of a mixture of petrol and crude soda. We were allowed to use just enough for a pot of tea and this, with some stale sandwiches, was all we had. My stepfather and Sungura worked on the lorry until well after dark, but without success so we made ourselves as comfortable as we could and tried to sleep.

Next morning my stepfather eventually persuaded the lorry to start and we went the rest of the way to Loliondo without further mishap. What caused the trouble of the fire we never knew, but our discomforts were soon forgotten. We arrived to a heart-warming reception, with two of the Loliondo Sikhs, one with his entire family, coming out into the road to greet us. Mr Jaghat Singh insisted that we have lunch with him, which suited us just fine, as, apart from the fact that we were ravenous, we were very partial to Sikh cooking. The other man was known as Borokata Singh. The story goes that he got his name because he was having an affair with his sister. She became pregnant and he was taken to court by their father. While being cross-examined by the magistrate, he pulled out a knife and cut off his penis, saying, 'That is what caused the trouble, not me!'

Ever since then he had been known by this name, borokata being Swahili for "cut penis."

Loliondo, in northern Tanganyika, is twenty miles from the Kenya border. It is five thousand feet above sea level and has an average annual rainfall of thirty inches. At this period it was inhabited mainly by three Masai clans. These were the Loita, the Purko and the Leitayo. There was also a scattering of the Kisongo clan. The area has some of the most fertile land in East Africa, but it was then utilised almost entirely by the nomadic Masai as seasonal grazing.

The actions and behaviour of the Masai are governed by two main factors: their clans and their age-groups. There are a number of clans and these were at one time based in particular areas, but over the years they have tended to intermingle and spread. They do, however, predominate in their original areas and, although the customs are basically the same, the clans practise many variations.

For example the Leitayo, which is based mainly in the Loliondo region, will not under any circumstances kill a cobra, nor will members of this clan allow anyone else to do so in their presence. The reason given for this is that when a woman is about to give birth, the cobra will come to her bed to comfort her. It is reputed to remain with her until the child is born and stays on for an extra day to see that all is well. It is then given a bowl of milk to drink after which it leaves. The Leitayo maintain, and are adamant about this, that the cobra will never attack a member of their clan as it too is a member of the clan.

The cobra is also related to other clans, namely the Ildaresero and the Elmagesen, and it behaves in the same way with them. There was an old man at Longido on the Tanzanian-Kenyan border who, it is claimed, could call a cobra at any time, and when travelling he was followed by cobras that insisted on protecting him.

The Ngidongi clan is that from which the witch-doctors come. The Masai believe very strongly that this clan has special hereditary powers and, by virtue of their profession, they are distributed throughout Masailand.

There are other clans, which the Masai do not accept as full-blooded Masai, but say they are throw-outs because they work with their hands. These are the weapon makers and include the Oldorobo, Lumbwa, Kaputi, Wakwavi and the Samburu tribe in the north of Kenya who are cut off from Masailand. Although their spearheads, knives and simis (long knives about three feet in length, in the shape of spearheads) are rather crude and made of very poor material (for they melt their own iron ore), today these weapons and tools are valued far higher by the Masai than the better implements made from steel produced in Birmingham, England, and sold for a tenth of the price.

Each of the clans has an associate animal member, and the relationship is very much the same as that one with the cobra. Some clans have three or four animal associates, all of which have a particular reason for being connected with that clan.

In order to avoid inbreeding the Masai may not marry within their clan. They are very strict about this. All the children of a man, irrespective of his wife's clan, belong to the father's clan. Generally speaking the young moran operates within the clan group. This, however, is not absolutely imperative as the age-groups are stronger than clans and have more meaning and authority.

Age-groups are approximately ten years apart. The oldest group in existence today with very few exceptions, if any, is the Oldewati, and on my reckoning the men in this group are somewhere between sixty-five and eighty years old. Then come the Oldoreto, followed by the Olkataten and then the Ilmirisho. This group is followed by the Olkalkal, and the Oljololek, which are the last named age-groups to date. The young morans who have not yet been named are called Ilbaranot, and will not be named until all in their age-group have been circumcised and been to the manyatta. They range in age from about fifteen to twenty-two.

In each age-group there is a leader who is usually appointed when they go to the moran manyatta. Under him there are junior leaders; and these men all normally hold their positions of authority within their age-groups throughout their lives. They are chosen for their popularity, feats of bravery, respect for their elders, physical appearance, and their general ability to outshine others in their day-to-day activities.

Until he is circumcised the young Masai is known as a layoni and from an early age is given small chores to perform. The young girl is called an ndito until she too is circumcised. During this period of the children's lives they are treated by the menfolk as unimportant and of no particular consequence, especially so the young layoni, who must be used but not considered except when he is working - looking after calves initially and later the cattle and sheep. He is not officially permitted to take part in any activity of sport or sex, but what he does on his own and away from the eyes of the elders, provided it does not in any way show disrespect, is his own business and is normally not interfered with. He is, however, expected to be efficient in these activities when the time comes for him to prove himself.

The ndito is slightly different in that when she reaches an age of approximately two years before puberty, the morans begin to take an interest in her. She then becomes a very important person, and is considered to be ready for sexual activity. This is accepted by all as being the correct behaviour, on condition that she does not have any sexual contact with a layoni, who is considered to be unclean. This, however, is often not the case as it happens that a girl may already have a longstanding friendship with a layoni before any moran became interested, although this is frowned upon by morans and elders. Few girls, if any, reach the age of ten as virgins.

The layoni, who has been brought up in the belief that sport, bravery, wealth and sex are the only things in life that matter, starts his sexual adventures at a very early age and invariably has a number of ndito girlfriends on the quiet, and can call on them behind the scenes. It is also accepted that he may, and often does, participate in sexual intercourse with a female donkey, although this is done well away from the notice of his superiors and is not admitted to. The elders may know what is going on, but it is thought to be of no importance as the donkey is a load carrier and useful for that purpose only. The same behaviour with a cow is forbidden as the cow verges on the sacred.

Loliondo district was administered by a young District Officer, usually on his second tour of service, or sometimes in the latter part of his first tour. The District Office or Boma was at the head of a valley, known to the Masai as Olgosorok. The bowl of the valley was covered with deep high-altitude forest-cedar, wild olive, podocarpus, loliondo and a variety of lesser trees. On either side were two fairly large mountain ranges, the slopes of which were open grassland with small clumps of forest scattered here and there. Behind the Boma were some of the most beautiful flower gardens to be seen in East Africa, and in front, running down into the valley, were the vegetable gardens. These were maintained by extra-mural prisoners under the direction of the police. A small forest stream, which started at a spring to the north of Loliondo, ran through the valley all year long and eventually joined the Waso River.

Besides the Boma, the only other buildings of any consequence were the District Officer's house and the police lines. The former consisted of three connected rondavels with a fourth in the garden as a guest house. The police lines were a quarter of a mile away with six rondavels housing the askaris - as policemen were called in those day - and their families. There was also a small office and a gaol, and surrounding the lines were several plots cultivated by the police families. This police unit, together with two veterinary guards and an untrained medical dresser, were the District Officer's main assistants.

Over the ridge lived the laibon, or witch-doctor. He could be an extremely useful member of the District Officer's team as he was also chief of the Kisongo tribe and had their full support. This clan was admittedly only a small one, but the laigwanan Leongiri was a member of the reigning witchdoctor family for all the Loliondo area. In addition he was a direct descendant of Sendeu who was then considered to be the foremost witch-doctor of all the Masai clans and of all time.

Some nine miles away from the District Office, over the hills, the Trichardt family had a farm, the only one within two hundred miles. From the Loliondo side this could be approached by a footpath, a fairly hazardous walk as the area was teeming with game, particularly buffalo. So usually when visiting the Trichardts we went via a twenty-mile ox-cart track which skirted the range down at Waso.

A couple of miles before one reached the District Office, on the edge of the forest, stood our shop and those of Jaghat Singh and

Borokata Singh. These Sikh families and the Trichardts were our only non-African neighbours, apart from the Government officials. Jaghat Singh owned a lorry and two other shops, one at Ol Bosimoru just inside the Kenya border, and the other at Malambo in Tanganyika. His trade was mainly with the Masai, using a barter system. They brought in hides and skins and exchanged them for sugar, blankets, matches, copper and steel wire, tobacco, red ochre, beads, pieces of tyre to make sandals, sharpening files, Birmingham-made spears, and sometimes maize meal.

My parents' shop was next door to Jaghat Singh's, and on the adjoining plot was our reconstructed house from Wasonyiro. It stood about twenty yards back from the road and behind it was the vegetable garden, while on the opposite side of the road was our flower garden, which fascinated the Masai as they could not understand why anyone should grow flowers just for looking at. The Europeans just thought it plain odd having it on the other side of the road.

Our trading activities were the same as Jaghat Singh's, and because of this a certain amount of friction grew up between us. One of the reasons was that we had a newer, and possibly slightly better, range of goods than the Sikh. But also in our shop we had the added interest for the Masai women (who did most of the shopping and bartering) of seeing a white woman for the first time.

My mother looked after the shop and my stepfather drove one of the lorries and purchased the stock. He would go to Narok in Kenya once or twice a month, which was a journey of a hundred and ten miles each way. It usually took him a day there and a day to return but if it was raining, or some other unforeseen circumstance cropped up, it could take a week or ten days for the round trip.

The District Officer at this time was a Captain Darley who had lost a leg during the 1914-18 war and described my stepfather as a 'Hun.' Darley had very little time for him and seemed to think that in some way my stepfather was directly responsible for the loss of his leg, but he got on well with my mother.

Captain Darley was soon succeeded by an exceptionally tall Australian, of six feet, seven-and-a-half inches. This outstanding man was on the first tour of his colonial service. His name was John Pride, one of the greatest characters I have ever met. He had been in the country for just over a year when he was sent to Loliondo. Before that he was stationed in Dar-es-Salaam and in the short time he had been there, he had learned KiSwahili well enough to pass as a local inhabitant. In order to do this efficiently, and to get information, he had taken unto himself three African "wives", one at Bagamoyo and the other two in different parts of Dar es Salaam. In the evening he would dress himself in a kanzu - a long flowing Arab robe - and with a red fez on his head, visit the houses of tax defaulters about whom he had been tipped off by his "wives". This caused quite an uproar, and in fact Pride's life was threatened. Therefore, he was hastily moved to Loliondo, but not before the local district treasury in Dar es Salaam was richer than it had been for some time.

It did not take John Pride long to establish a reputation for himself among the people of Loliondo. The arrival of a new District Officer was something of an event and called for celebrations. So the night that John came Captain Darley invited the new Veterinary Officer and my parents to meet him - but before Pride set foot in the house Darley took the precaution of banishing his African mistress to the back quarters. She was a good-looking Chagga girl and he was not taking any chances with John Pride around. However, John arrived with a most attractive young African lady whom he introduced as his girlfriend from the coast. She was smartly dressed in the coastal fashion and when asked to have a drink, replied in perfect English that she would like a whisky with water. She had several of these without any apparent ill effect. Her name was Fatuma and after this evening often visited our house, becoming very friendly with my mother in whom she confided all her troubles.

On the next day a second party was held at the District Office. To this were invited the Sikhs, the group of the previous night, the Trichardts and Leongiri, the laigwanan, with his entourage. This consisted of two sub-chiefs, a number of junior chiefs, clan leaders and witch-doctors. There were four hundred morans in full battle attire and countless women and children. The Masai had encamped half a mile from the Boma and were slaughtering animals they had brought along for the festivities. They also provided themselves with a great deal of locally brewed beer.

After John had met everyone at the Boma, the Masai morans invited him to join them in their feast. He declined for that day as he had matters to discuss with the elders, but he promised he would visit them the next day. From the first he struck everyone as being an open-hearted, straightforward and uninhibited man, friendly and at ease with all. He was only twenty-five years old at the time.

True to his word, the next day John visited the morans, joining in with their festivities and taking their food and drink. He seemed to have a great way with the Masai, and particularly with the morans who were not always easy to get on with, and he was accepted by them from the start. They called him Ngong'u meaning "eyes" as he wore glasses. He was a frequent visitor to our house as my stepfather was considered quite an authority on what was happening in the neighbourhood, and John would consult him on various matters. I got to know him very well and we became good friends.

It was about this time that I first met Matanda, a Masai layoni some three years my senior. He told me he was soon to be circumcised and would no longer be a layoni but a moran, destined to kill many lions. This was boasting, of course, as he was far too young, but even so I was impressed. He had come, he said, to bring my mother a gift of meat in return for having treated his sister for sore eyes. I asked where the meat had come from and he told me it was from an olpul (a Masai meat festival) a mile away down the river. He insisted that I should go back with him and I was only too delighted to do so.

CHAPTER SEVEN

THE MASAI MALE

I FOUND THE OLPUL FASCINATING. It was my first introduction to the Masai way of cooking meat over an open fire, and I stayed there until late afternoon when my parents sent for me to return home. During the next week I was there every day and was sorry when it ended, but Matanda assured me there were other olpuls going on in the area and he would fetch me when any of his friends slaughtered an animal. We saw a lot of each other after this and I met a number of his layoni friends.

It was due entirely to my friendship with Matanda over many years that I learnt to speak Masai and gained a knowledge of their habits, customs and beliefs. When a Masai women is seven or eight months' pregnant, she takes a specially prepared calabash with hide sewn along it on both sides. Directly into it she milks a cow with no deformities or blemishes. It must also have no white spot of any kind on the head or tail. The woman and a young maiden from her manyatta then dress in their best garments and adornments and smear themselves with red ochre, making attractive designs on their faces. Carrying the calabash of milk they go to the nearest spring where they top the milk up with clear water. It does not matter how far the nearest spring may be - only spring water can be used for this purpose. On returning home they take a sip of the mixture and all the young children in the manyatta are given a taste too.

The cow is now the official property of the unborn child. If the child should be stillborn or die, the cow must not be presented to another unborn baby as it now holds a bad omen. The expectant mother again collects milk from the same cow and boils the root of the seki tree, which is cooled before being mixed with the milk. This is sipped as before.

The seki tree is sacred, and if at any time a young boy or moran, or even a group of morans, are beaten in a fight or battle, an individual or the leader may ask for the protection of the seki tree. Defeat is thereby admitted and the fight or battle will cease immediately without any disgrace to either side. The logic here is clear. The Masai maintain that every battle has to be won and lost, by one side or the other.

When the child is born, the midwife calls for the layonis whose job it is to extract blood from the cattle, and she rubs a little butter on their heads. She then instructs them to take blood from a bullock if the baby is a boy, from a heifer if it is a girl. In either case the layonis will catch the animal and strike the vein with a specially prepared arrow, but they will only collect the blood for a male baby. A woman or girl will collect it if the baby is female. Watching these proceedings, all the people of the manyatta will then know the sex of the newborn child.

Until the afterbirth has been removed from the hut, and this can only be done during the hours of darkness, no man may enter. Nor may anyone drink milk or water. If the child is born in the night, the afterbirth cannot be moved until the following night. No woman in the hut is permitted to partake of any food or water from the hut, which is considered unclean, as is the whole manyatta, until the removal of the afterbirth. As soon as this has been done, it is the responsibility of the father to provide food for everyone. A sheep is slaughtered in the entrance to the hut for the women and, depending on the father's wealth, either an ox or a goat is killed for the men to eat.

When the boy child is very small and still being breast-fed, the mother starts to force back his foreskin, squeezing milk from her breast on to the head of the penis to ease the strain. This is done every two or three days until her breasts dry out.

When he is about six years of age, the tops of both the boy's ears are pierced and, when they are healed, his mother will make him a fancy ring with beads and bits of metal for each ear. He will wear these embenyets or olkangalai until his circumcision. Later, if he wishes, he will have two more holes pierced halfway down the ears. This is done by his layoni friends and is entirely optional, but anyone who does not have these holes may not attend the orgesher or eunoto - the ceremony in which the morans become elders. A man without these two extra holes may celebrate and will become an elder, but he may not attend the actual orgesher, which is a very select, very secret ceremony.

At about the time the boys have the middle of their ears pierced, they themselves cut out one another's light cord joining the foreskin to the head of the penis. This is done with the sharp edge of the bark of split bracken. When erect with the foreskin forced back, the penis is straight and this is supposed to make circumcision easier.

Next, the boy's father orders that the lobe of his right ear be pierced. A small hole is made and a tiny wooden wedge smeared with fat is inserted. When it is healed the wedge is removed and replaced with a bigger one. This is repeated, with bigger and bigger wedges, until the boy is satisfied with the size. This is usually when a piece of wood about four inches in diameter can be fitted into the hole. After a year the left ear is treated in the same way.

During all this time the young layoni learns from his own experience the skills of livestock management. He has become a competent herder, can diagnose animal diseases and knows their treatment. He is also able to castrate steers and slaughter animals for food. He can deliver a calf in a difficult birth without help, he knows how to behave at the different stages of his life, and what his responsibilities are towards the tribe. He has also taught himself the art of combat against wild animals and other enemies.

When the layoni has an opportunity of proving himself amongst the other layonis, he will do so; and in an emergency where there are no morans nearby he will also step to the fore. So from time to time his abilities come to the notice of his elders. For example, during his older years as a layoni, while out herding, the cattle may be attacked by predators. Normally he would have to send for help from the morans, and this would be considered the correct action to take. On the other hand, should he deal with the situation himself successfully, it would be to his credit. Often a boy is killed in the attempt to prove his worth. He will try to achieve recognition not only in the field of battle but also on the sports ground and with his favours amongst the nditos, any exceptional feat again going to his credit. When the time comes for circumcision and the choosing of clan and group leaders, these points will be taken into consideration. All this is extremely tough for him as he is still, in the eyes of the morans and elders, of no consequence.

The next stage is his circumcision, and this is a very big event in the life of the Masai male. It usually takes place between the ages of fifteen and twenty-three. He is either called by his father and told that he is now ready for circumcision, or if he feels himself that he is ready and his father has not broached the subject, he may go to him and suggest it. If his father is satisfied and does not require him particularly for odd jobs, he will give his consent, providing the olpiron, the fire-stick, is not broken.

The word olpiron has two meanings. Firstly, it is an actual stick similar to an arrow and about the same size. When this stick is symbolically broken, no further circumcisions may take place, and they may only be carried out when the olpiron is bound with strips of gut and therefore repaired.

Secondly, the name olpiron is given to the relationship between alternate circumcision groups. Therefore, the men who are two age-groups above those being circumcised, are their olpirons, as those youngsters are themselves the older men's olpirons.

The fire-stick is broken by the elder morans to signal the end of a series of circumcisions. This is always done to protect the very young and to ensure that not too many layonis are circumcised in one group. These elder morans then become the olpirons to the layonis they have withheld from circumcision. It may be seven to ten years before the fire-stick is repaired. The breakers will also be the ones to decide when it may be repaired. Once they have given their approval and it is bound, it is handed down to the last group of morans circumcised. This gives licence to parents and the layonis to make their circumcision arrangements. Under no circumstances may male circumcision take place while the fire-stick remains broken.

Instructors are appointed from among the layonis' olpirons and it is their job to initiate the layonis in behaviour and prepare and approve them for the ceremony. The instructors will call assemblies of layonis in different areas and individual boys will be asked to produce an ox, a blanket, and the ingredients for making beer for their instructors. When the time is considered right, the layonis are taken to the witch-doctor and permission is requested to hold a ngipataa, a celebration to draw attention to their uncircumcised state.

The witch-doctor now sends the layonis to an elder who also has a boy in this group and he will order his son to paint nine of his friends for the ngipataa. Their clothes are removed for all to see that they are uncircumcised, and their bodies are painted in stripes with whitewash, red ochre and ground-up charcoal. They tie bells to their legs and wear head-dresses of feathers. As soon as the nine boys have been painted, the others too are daubed by anyone present and they themselves help one another. After feasting on meat and milk, the instructor leads them to a pond, which they surround, leaving a gap to the north for Ngai, their god. At midnight they start to dance, and it is said that lions and ostriches come to join them. The ostriches circle clockwise round the boys and the lions move in the opposite direction, roaring all night. The dancing goes on, with the youths making as much noise as possible, until they become tired and sleep until the sun is well up before returning home. A second ngipataa will be held later, after which circumcisions begin.

While these overall preparations are being carried out, the individual layoni and his father will also make their own private arrangements. The father contacts other elders with sons of approximately the same age, and mentions that he is considering having his boy circumcised during the next few months. A date is decided upon, and he will obtain sugar and up to fifteen gallons of honey for making beer, which will be brewed by the women of the manyatta. An ox is selected and slaughtered, and the circumciser, who is always of the Oldorobo tribe, will arrive on the day arranged. He will receive one medium-sized goat for each circumcision performed.

The day before circumcision the young layoni, accompanied by one of the morans, goes to the nearest forest, which in many cases may be ten or fifteen miles away, and cuts an olive sapling about ten feet long. All the branches except those at the top are removed and it is carried back to the manyatta where it is planted twenty yards or so from the gate and tied to a forked olive stick to keep it, upright. At the same time the boy is given a special axe, called an ndolu, which is placed in an earthenware bowl with water. This is put beside the sapling and is there purely to signify to passers-by that a circumcision is about to take place.

Festival hides are spread inside the manyatta for the elders to squat on while joining in the celebration. Here they sit and drink and eat meat brought to them by the morans. The meat is cut up and cooked by the morans at their olpul some distance away, where no circumcised woman is allowed as it is forbidden for such a female to see the meat at that stage. It is divided into three lots: that for the elders, which is carried to them already cooked (and can be seen by women); meat for the women and children, some of which is cooked and some raw; and meat for the morans, which remains at the olpul and must not, under any circumstances, be seen by a circumcised woman.

Some morans may wish to join in the drinking. If so, they go to the manyatta, returning to the olpul to eat. No moran will drink to excess as it is considered to be bad manners to be drunk in front of his elders. He must also bear in mind that if he is too drunk and unable to perform sexually, he may well be ostracised by the girls and his moran friends.

On the morning of the circumcision, the layoni uses the water from the bowl containing the axe to bathe his entire body. He then sits down on a hide placed on the left-hand side of his father's gate to the manyatta. Elders and morans congregate and a chosen elder, of the same age-group as the layoni's father, sits down behind the young man. He places his arm around the layoni's belly and spreads his legs out flat on either side. The layoni's legs are inside the elder's, with the knees up and splayed out. He clutches the undersides of his knees with his hands and bends his head forward in order to watch the operation. This he must do throughout.

The Oldorobo squats in front of the layoni with his home-cast knife, pushes the foreskin back from the head of the penis, and cuts round the inner layer of the foreskin. He parts the inner layer from the outer, making the whole foreskin about four inches long, and cuts a slit across the outer layer above the head of the penis, which is then pushed through the cut. The inner layer is then pared away, leaving the outer layer hanging down below the head of the penis. This, which the Masai call ndelelia, is believed by them to give a girl more pleasure during intercourse and is also supposed to protect the new moran against venereal disease.

If the young moran flinches in any way during the operation, he disgraces not only himself but all his family. He may be summarily thrashed, with the ceremony coming to an abrupt end, to be carried out at a later date, or he may be held down and forcibly circumcised, in which case he will be in disgrace for the rest of his life.

If there are two full brothers, the younger one will sit on a separate hide to the left, and the circumciser, having completed the operation on the elder boy, will move on to him. The Oldorobo will then proceed to the next gate or the next manyatta. He may do anything up to twenty circumcisions in a day.

The new moran, covered with a hide, is carried by the elder, who sat behind him, to his mother's hut where he is laid on a bed, and bleeding is allowed to continue without hindrance. He is left to his mother's ministrations, while the people of his manyatta celebrate his new status well into the night.

The next morning the moran is bathed in warm water - probably the last water bath he will ever have. When the cattle are let out of the manyatta, the olive sapling is taken away and the hole it stood in is filled with milk to remove any evil spirits from the moran's body. Every two or three days over the next few months he will be anointed with fat from the ox slaughtered at the time of his circumcision.

During his convalescence, the moran will feed on a milk-and-blood mixture with a little mutton fat added. Fresh blood is drawn every day from a healthy ox by piercing the jugular vein with a specially made arrow-head, half an inch in diameter. Fixed on the arrow is a small ball of bees' wax to prevent too deep a penetration. The blood, about half a gallon at a time, is drained into a calabash and whipped immediately to stop congealing. It is then mixed with heated milk and fat. After the blood has been drawn, the cow's vein is pinched together with two fingers until bleeding stops. An animal will not be bled more than once a season as a rule, and certainly not before four weeks have elapsed since the previous time.

Among some of the clans, if the newly circumcised moran had in the past made indecent suggestions to a circumcised woman or a female of his own clan, she may now come forward and make advances to him, simply to cause him pain. This can extend the period of recovery for the moran quite considerably; but in the majority of clans, if the matter is brought to the attention of the elders, the young man is given a good whipping and all is forgotten.

The patient is usually sufficiently recovered in a fortnight to walk about and go bird hunting. Surprisingly enough, complications very seldom set in although the conditions under which the operation is carried out and the moran convalesces, leave much to be desired from a hygienic point of view.

Morans circumcised at about the same time form little groups and go visiting one manyatta after another, and may not return home for as long as two months or more. During this time the new morans go armed with arrows, which have heads of bee's, wax the size of an egg. These are used for killing birds without damaging them. These birds they skin from the back to the base of the head and stuff with grass, all without impairing the feathers. The birds are affixed to head-dresses, and the object is to fill them with as many varieties of bird as possible. The head-dresses sometimes hold as many as seventy-five birds and may take from a couple of months to a year to complete. The birds are tied on while the flesh in the head is still fresh, but for some unknown reason they never seem to rot. The young moran is often judged by the girls on the quality and rarity of the birds in his head-dress, and this can give him prestige within his own age-group and among the elders.

The moran now feeds on plain milk and fat only. He is not permitted to shave any part of his body during this period, which may last six months or longer, but when the time comes for him to shed his head-dress there is a short ceremony at which he is shaved of all hair. He disposes of his previous dress and covers himself with red ochre, putting on a new loin-cloth (this is not a loin-cloth in the true sense of the word. It is a piece of cloth wrapped round the body and tied on one shoulder, rather like a toga but very short and just covering the buttocks. In the past it would have been made from calf- or goat-skin). He then goes on to an olpul for the first time as a moran, with half a dozen others and usually several young nditos and layonis whose job it is to carry and do errands at the olpul.

The moran's existence is now dictated to a large extent by his age-group. These change every seven to ten years and when one group moves up, a new group is formed through circumcision. There are always two moran groups in being at the same time. These are the older "working morans" and the younger ones who do no work but spend their days and nights enjoying themselves, in particular stealing cattle and raiding. If, however, there is a war the older morans lead and direct the battle with the younger men joining in and helping, but only if they have been shaved. They are not permitted to take part otherwise.

When the older morans are satisfied that sufficient young men and boys have been circumcised and that those remaining are not yet old enough for circumcision, their group will break the olpiron, the fire-stick.

Shortly after the young morans have been to their first round of olpuls, their leader (who is the clan leader in this case) will call all the young men to the moran manyatta - the training camp for the warriors. These are always built in the same areas but never on the same site twice. Some of the warrior manyattas are very large, holding up to two hundred and fifty huts; and they are seldom, if ever, surrounded by thorn or brushwood.

Once the moran has been called, he immediately informs his mother and gives her the name of the asanja (sweetheart) he wishes to accompany him. His mother will tell the girl, but if she is already committed to go with someone else, his mother will ask his second choice.

His mother will now call on the mother of the senior moran and on a given date all the mothers will go with the leader's mother to the site of the new warrior camp and choose the positions of their huts. Building will start and when the women have completed the huts, they and the asanjas, together with the morans, will move into the new manyatta. They will take sufficient donkeys to carry the loads and enough cattle for milk and slaughter for the period of their stay, normally about two years.

The mother's sole purpose will be to tend to her son's needs and make him comfortable. This duty is sometimes carried out by the asanja if she is not too young, or if the moran's mother is dead, but usually the girl is taken solely for his pleasure.

The morans now begin their warrior training seriously. They are formed into battle groups under junior leaders, and it is in these groups that they will go out hunting. The various clans have their own methods of hunting different types of game, and one of the more spectacular of these is the five-man lion hunt. There is a spear-man (who, if he survives, will get the credit for the kill), a tail-man, a shield-man and two reserves for the spear- and tail-men. The reserves position themselves slightly away from the others, but move forward as soon as the lion attacks.

The method here is for the shield-man, carrying only his shield and a few stones in his right hand, to go forward, attract the attention of the lion, and entice it to attack him. When the lion charges he bends down, covering himself with his shield, while the tail-man comes in from the blind side of the lion and grabs its tail. This must be done very fast and accurately, as the man carries no weapon whatsoever and relies entirely on the drag of the tail. Once he has firm hold of the tail, the spear-man lunges in and spears the lion in the shoulder.

If the tail-man is unsuccessful, his reserve will move to help him; and in the same way, if the spear-man's thrust is not totally effective, his reserve will step in and complete the killing. If the first man punctures the skin of the lion, irrespective of whether it was the fatal wound, or contributed at all to the death of the animal, he is credited with the kill and will have the mane for his head-dress. In the event of him being killed his reserve will get the credit. The shield-man is usually one who has already achieved a kill, whereas the tail-man will be the next to have the honour of being spear-man. He is the most likely man to be turned on by the lion, very often losing his life. Although he may not get the kudos for having killed the lion, if he has held the tail with strength and courage the prestige obtained by doing so could well place him above all others in the manyatta.

The Masai do not hunt for the pot, but will kill lion, leopard, buffalo and rhinoceros, not only as a demonstration of their manhood and courage, but also for the specific purpose of obtaining leather for shields and skins for ceremonial use and as head-dresses.

The morans will also begin their raiding careers at this time, for they, and especially the laigwanans, are very anxious to let off steam and will take any opportunity they can to prove themselves. The witch-doctors grow rich from the consulting fees they charge and, in order to attract business, will continually advise the morans to go off on raids.

In the early stages the raids are carried out close to home against other Masai clans, usually at night but sometimes during the day when the cattle are grazing. A junior laigwanan with one or two dozen followers may go out to steal a few head of cattle and will take the animals to an olpul for slaughter. Once a group has been successful a couple of times, it may invite another group to join it or, if big enough, go on a raid against one of the neighbouring tribes. Major fighting is avoided on these occasions, and the morans will not normally attack a large force. Livestock gained on the raids is taken back to the home manyatta to be divided equally amongst the morans, but the laigwanans will get a greater share. These sorties are not to be confused with war raids directed and organised by elder morans.

Often when out on a raid the young morans may be called upon to participate in tribal battles led by the elder morans. And it is at this time that the competitive spirit between the battle groups and individuals is built up to fever pitch, all trying to outdo one another in sport, sex and battle. Consequently serious fights can often flare up.

In the evenings a big fire is lit in the middle of the manyatta and this is tended by the women while the morans and young girls dance and sing. No drink is permitted at a warrior camp. As the evening draws to an end the morans pile their knobkerries in a large heap and each girl then picks one out, the owner of which will spend the night with her.

The girls, like the morans, may or may not gain reputations at these manyattas for their sexual skills, and these reputations are very important to them as they will remain with them for the rest of their active sexual lives.

For many years both the former colonial governments and present independent governments in Kenya and Tanzania have been disturbed by the problem of the Masai warrior manyattas, and have tried to ban the custom, but no one has ever put forward an alternative for the morans during this stage of their lives. In my opinion, unless an effective alternative for the moran to let off steam is found, it would be better to let the present system continue. While the moran manyatta continues, cattle thieving and raiding of other tribes will remain a manly sport, but if the system is destroyed these people will be turned into unpleasant criminals.

CHAPTER EIGHT

THE OLPUL

ONE DAY MATANDA TOLD ME that his father had sold my father an ox to be trained as a work ox, and begged me to ask my father not to harm the animal, as he was very fond of it. This was the first indication I had that my parents intended to start farming. I mentioned the matter to my mother later and she told me that they had bought a large number of animals, and hoped to get more, for training as trek oxen. They needed these, she explained, as they had applied for a thousand acres of land in the vicinity of our house and shop. There was every possibility that they would get the land as both the Masai and the Administration were in favour of the idea. A farm in the area, it was hoped, would help feed the Masai in famine years, which were all too frequent.

Matanda's father had wanted to move his manyatta closer to us, its present site being three miles away, but had been told he could not do this as the land was being given to my stepfather, so he had to stay where he was. Matanda and I were disappointed about this as it meant we still had to make a long walk to see each other. However, there was so much going on that we soon forgot all about it.

Within a short while work began on a cattle boma, or corral, for our ox teams, and Matanda and I took a personal interest in the building of this, as usual getting in everyone's way. Sungura told us his uncle and two friends were arriving soon from Kenya, to be in charge of the cattle and their training; and on the next trip from Narok our lorry brought these men, together with yokes, chains, and yards and yards of cured hide cut into strips known as riems.

The training that followed was not exactly kind to the animals, but was the usual method. First, the oxen had chains fastened round their necks, and these they carried for two weeks after which they were trained to carry riems round their horns. When the oxen became used to the chains and riems, they were put in a yoke in twos and made to walk about together, but without being led. This came next, with a man walking in front leading them; at the same time a chain was attached to the yoke and was dragged along the ground behind. As soon as they were quiet enough Matanda and I occupied ourselves with this task. The next step was to tie a log to the chain, which they pulled. When a pair of oxen was accustomed to pulling a log, they were linked up to another pair, and so on until a team of sixteen was inspanned or harnessed. During the training, animals were selected for their particular adaptabilities, to be team leaders or rear oxen. When a team was fully trained the oxen were capable of leading themselves, even at night, with only the driver in charge.

When ploughing started on our farm some time later, we had six teams of sixteen head each, and eventually we built up to twelve teams. Each would work for four hours, then another team would take over, and so on. All went well until rinderpest struck the area and we lost sixty per cent of our oxen. My stepfather then decided that to use cattle for ploughing in a place like Loliondo was too unreliable, as the Masai were continually moving their stock about and so spreading disease. Also cattle rustling was rife. We were therefore not surprised to see, when my stepfather returned from one of his jaunts to Nairobi, a Farmall tractor on the back of the lorry. This proved to be a great asset, and in the initial stages it took the place of three teams of oxen, working twice as fast. We still continued to use some oxen, although the main work was now being done by tractor.

The first season for us at Loliondo turned out to be particularly bad for moran raids on cattle. I was shortly to find out where at least some of the stolen cattle were disappearing to. Matanda and I were out one day in the forest with two other layonis when we came across cattle tracks. It looked as if there was only one animal accompanied, as far as we could make out from the footprints, by five people. We and the three dogs that were always with us followed the tracks for two and a half hours, deep into the forest. After crossing a small ravine and trying to pick up the spoor again on the other side, we heard sounds of chopping.

We thought it might be honey hunters so we followed the direction of the noise, only to find that an olpul was being held in a cave. This was where the animal we had tracked had been brought for slaughter by the morans.

We were spotted immediately, and one of the morans asked, 'What are you youngsters doing here? You know that children are not allowed to wander in the forest. It is dangerous!'

Just then a moran we knew appeared, and Matanda told him we were hunting.

'What are you hunting?'

'Anything,' I replied for him, then continued, 'what are you all doing?'

We knew exactly what they were doing by now. We could smell the roasting meat.

'Well,' said the first moran, 'you had better all go now as it will soon be dark.' And to my companions he said, 'You should not have brought the European boy so far into the forest.' He then told one of the morans to escort us back.

'They have killed a stolen ox,' Matanda whispered to me.

'We know what you are doing,' I shouted. 'You stole an ox, and if you chase us away we shall report you!'

'All right, come in,' said the first moran. 'But remember! Keep your eyes closed and your mouths shut, or you will lose them!' A Masai expression meaning "mind your own business".

The ox had been killed that morning, and we learned that not only had it been stolen from a Masai manyatta, but from the father of one of those now eating it.

We were given our fill of roasted meat and also herb soup, which we imagined would make us very brave. I was taken into a corner by a moran and lectured about "splitting" and Matanda was told very sternly that if I did, the consequences would be unpleasant for him. I assured the moran that I would not think of doing such a thing – I was too anxious to come again, and asked him if we could. He said, 'If you keep quiet, yes.'

We left with the three dogs, also well fed on scraps, and set off for home. Suddenly the dogs started to bark and raced off ahead of us. We followed them and found they had surrounded a wild pig. Matanda shouted, 'Don't get too near! The tusks are very dangerous.' But I was too excited to take any notice and dashed forward. Just at that moment the pig broke loose, knocked me down and ran over me. Luckily it did no damage apart from a few bruises. The dogs had tasted blood and would not give up the chase. We followed for as long as we could, but had to give up as we could not keep pace with them. However, just after we stopped we heard the dogs barking again so, tired as we were, we carried on. This time we were better organised and as the dogs held down the pig we killed it with a spear belonging to one of the layonis. After this, I got a spear of my own.

This was our first sizeable kill so we were very excited about it and proud of ourselves. It was getting dark and we were still four miles from home, and we should have got off as quickly as possible, but we could not bear to leave the pig and decided to take it with us as evidence of our success. To do this we cut an eight-foot pole and tied it between the pig's legs after cutting off its head. We then strapped the legs together around the pole and carried the pig home, accompanied, we thought, by all three dogs. But when we eventually arrived at my house a couple of hours later, we discovered we had only two dogs and they were covered in what we assumed to be pig blood. We examined them in the lamplight however and found they were bleeding from tusk wounds.

While my layoni friends faded into the background, I proceeded to get a good dressing down, the first of many to follow for very much the same reasons: Why was I late? Why had I gone out in the first place without saying where I was going? What did I mean by taking the dogs and allowing them to be so badly gored? And so on. At this moment the missing dog, Simba, arrived in a poor state, which made matters worse for me. He had a large hole in his side, which appeared to go right through to his chest.

For the next two days I remained at home, but Matanda visited our new friends at the olpul and told them I had been in trouble with my family. He told them too that I had kept the secret of the olpul, and as a reward I was sent a large piece of meat wrapped in fresh forest leaves. When my mother asked where the beef had come from I told her I had got it from a completely different source than an olpul. I do not think she believed me, as she repeated her question several times.

The next day we heard about an animal that had been stolen from a manyatta ten miles away, so on the fourth day the four of us again went to visit the morans at the olpul, taking two of the dogs who were fighting fit once more. Simba had to remain behind as he was still recovering from his encounter with the wild pig.

We were accepted this time at the olpul, chatting with the morans and filling ourselves with meat. They told us that the tribal police had found out about the ox but had been bought off. By now the morans seemed to trust us, and took us into their confidence. They said they planned to steal another animal from the manyatta of one of their number, which they would kill at a place ten miles away, and they told us where the olpul was to be held. When I asked them why they stole from their own relations they told me that the family of the moran concerned were quite rich but were too mean to let them have any cattle to slaughter as was the custom. So, as the other morans at the olpul had supplied their share from their family herds, what could they do but steal an animal from the mean parent, in order to save the son embarrassment?

I then asked, why not steal from a stranger? They explained that as the olpul season was coming to an end, it was hardly worth the effort of making a raid into Sukumaland. They might end up with more cattle than they needed, which would be more of a liability than an asset. I then suggested that they steal locally, but not from their families; this idea was not acceptable either as such a theft would be treated seriously and the people from whom they stole would go to great lengths to catch them. I obviously did not understand the system of stealing for an olpul, and as I did not want to get into trouble again for being late, I set off for home with Matanda and the two dogs, leaving behind the other layonis.

About two days later the first aeroplane I had ever seen appeared in the sky and circled round and round overhead. It was two o'clock in the afternoon; my stepfather shouted to everyone in Swahili, 'Get down to the mbuga, all of you, as fast as possible!' And to my mother he called out for paraffin.

'How much? She asked.

'Oh, two or three bottles will do.'

We all congregated on the flat, about six hundred yards from the house, and hastily collected grass and anything else that would burn, piling it up at four points. We then poured the paraffin on these heaps and set them alight. I did not at the time understand what this was all about, but I learned later that these fires were signals indicating the direction of the wind and where the plane should land. When the fires were lit the tiny Leopard Moth landed quickly and safely.

By this time about two hundred people had assembled on our improvised landing strip, for such a strange phenomenon had never been seen in those parts before. The District Officer, the Veterinary Officer, the Indian shopkeepers and uncountable Masai together with their wives and children were there to goggle and wonder at this amazing sight. The pilot, my parents and the two Administration men went off to our house, but I remained with my Masai friends to discuss the happenings of the afternoon and to inspect the plane, which was being guarded by an askari. Someone started the story that the aeroplane had come from heaven, and that unless it was shown hospitality on a large scale it would return whence it came and leave behind bad luck.

That evening three head of cattle arrived for the pilot who insisted he could not possibly accept them as he could neither eat all three nor take them with him. But the Masai were firm in their determination that he could not leave under any circumstances until they had had an opportunity to show him hospitality. Also, they said, the animals would have to be killed, even if the meat was left to the hyenas. My stepfather then took this difficult matter in hand and assured the elders that if the morans turned up the following day in their war dress, a celebration would be held on the farm and the wishes of all would be satisfied.

No less than twelve head of cattle were slaughtered on the next day, and the people gorged themselves on the meat. The morans and women danced to the incessant hooting of game horns and the children laughed and squealed tirelessly. For three days the merrymaking continued and the Masai encampment looked as though it had been there for ever. The women and girls tended the cooking fires and kept the gourds filled with beer. The enthusiasm of the Masai, not only to have a party but to keep it going, was boundless.

Early on the third day the pilot took off to a cheering crowd, on his way to South Africa. This episode was talked about by the Masai for many years, but, the tale was not believed by those who had not actually seen the plane.

Unfortunately I am unable to remember the exact date that this took place, and have not been able to trace the name of the pilot or his progress. At the time I was very much like my Masai friends: thunderstruck by the whole affair and more interested in the immediate spiritual aspects of the incident than the facts.

About thirty years later I visited the same area in my Cessna 180 and took Matanda and half a dozen others, in turn, up for flights around Loliondo; we discussed the arrival of the Leopard Moth so many years before and laughed at the effect this visit had had on everybody, who had then believed that the plane was a spirit. When I suggested that they might have a party and slaughter cattle for me, Matanda remarked that I may be very clever to fly my own plane, but I was certainly no god - merely a straightforward human being like everyone else. A sure sign of the changing times.

CHAPTER NINE

THE LONG WALK

ONE EVENING WHEN JOHN PRIDE was having a drink with my parents he appeared suddenly to notice me and said, 'Hey, young scallywag! How would you like to go on safari with me for three months?'

I was not too certain of John yet, and did not know if he meant it.

'What's all this about a safari?' my mother broke in.

'In about ten days' time I'm going on a wagon safari, collecting taxes and having a good look at the district on foot. It will take about three months, and I thought young David might like to come with me. It will give him something to do.'

My mother said, 'That's very nice of you, John, but I'm sure you don't want the child around you all that time.'

'He can bring his layoni friend with him,' John went on. 'I'm sure he won't get in my way and they'll keep each other company. If he does annoy me he'll soon get his ears pinned back.'

I begged my mother to let me go, and a few days later she told John I could go with him, providing he really meant it and that he would not hesitate to discipline me if necessary. Before the great day arrived I was in a fever of excitement, but when I told Matanda he could come too, he took it very calmly and said 'Good show' in Masai, or words to that effect.

'You had better ask your parents' permission, then,' I told him.

'Why should I?' he answered. 'It is nothing to do with them; I shall just tell them I am going.'

'Well, they may need you to look after cattle or something.'

'There are many other layonis in our manyatta whose fathers' work for my father. Why do you ask?' he said, 'Did you have to get your parents' permission?'

'Yes, I did, and they very nearly did not let me go.' I could see that Matanda was quite shocked that I had had to have parental approval.

On the morning of our departure, long before daylight, I heard a knock on my window, which woke me. It was Matanda. I got up, hurriedly put on my clothes and went to open the front door.

'What's going on?' my stepfather shouted from the next room.

I told him that Matanda had arrived and we were ready to go. He groaned and pointed out that it was only four in the morning and John would not be coming past the house until nine, and would we kindly be quiet and go to sleep. I let Matanda in and went back to bed while he slept in a chair. I noticed that all he had with him was a calabash, his knife attached to his belt and a loin-cloth. He had left his spear stuck in the ground outside our front door.

'Is that all you are taking, Matanda?'

'What else should I take?'

'Well, we are going on safari for three months, you know,' I answered.

'I cannot see that I could need anything more, however long I am going to be away.'

This stumped me because I realised then that there was in fact nothing else a Masai would need.

At ten John arrived, followed by a man carrying a gun. He said he was going on ahead as he had a meeting at Waso three miles away. I could either walk with him or wait for the wagon. I decided to wait as I wanted to make sure my things were safely loaded.

Presently the wagon came creaking along the dusty road, pulled by a team of sixteen trek oxen and followed by two spare teams, which were being herded. The wagon stopped and the herded oxen carried on. My things were thrown on board and my mother had a few words with John's cook, probably about me. I said my goodbyes and we moved off, Matanda and I striding out beside the wagon and full of high spirits.

After about ten miles the ox team was changed while John and I lunched on tea and sandwiches (Matanda preferred to eat at manyattas en route, although he did enjoy an occasional cup of tea). A further six miles of trekking brought us to a river where we pitched camp for the night. There was no manyatta in the vicinity so we did not have the usual large numbers of Masai women and children as spectators. John arrived not long after and called everyone together to tell us exactly what each person's duties were to be. He said this was the pattern to be carried out at every camp that we came to and that he did not want to have to repeat his instructions daily.

Martin, the Nandi head cattle-man, was in charge of all the trek oxen and the wagon. With him were five other Nandi and fifteen Sonjo tribesmen who were employed as general labourers. At this first camp two of the Nandi were sent off to water and herd the oxen while half the Sonjo gang were put to work to make a small enclosure of brushwood for the cattle to sleep in. Saidi, John's cook, was in charge of the camp, helped by another servant and by one of the Government messengers. The latter was sent to collect wood and water, but he in turn delegated his duties to two of the Sonjo and made them do it. Saidi waged a continual battle with this idle individual who was very adept at avoiding any task.

The senior head messenger, who accompanied John wherever he

went, dealt with the tentage. This he did very efficiently throughout the safari. He was a fierce-looking Nandi and carried a long hippo-hide whip, which he used without hesitation when he thought it necessary. Matanda and I regarded him with great respect. Having measured the length of his whip, we kept that distance from him at all times.

John's chair and table were placed under a convenient tree for his meeting with the Masai elders. These were held whenever we were in camp and as a rule lasted about an hour and a half. The same procedure was followed throughout the safari. Messengers were sent out in the mornings in advance of the main party to inform the elders in the various manyattas we expected to pass through and where we hoped to camp. If anyone wished to see the District Officer he would know where to go and at what time. A man not coming punctually would simply have to catch us up at the next stop. John would .close the meetings when it grew dark and after supper we all sat round the fire and listened to stories. Matanda and I would then take ourselves off to bed in the wagon, where we slept every night on the safari.

On the second day we set out very early, having only had tea and no breakfast. We carried on until midday when we halted to change the team of oxen and eat a cold lunch. We then went on until about four o'clock or the nearest water point where we stopped for the night. This was the routine we followed throughout. We tried always to stop near waterholes or rivers, but sometimes owing to the distance we took one-and-a-half to two days to reach the next water point. On two occasions we had to travel through the night because of this problem; we then used all three teams of oxen on four-hour shifts, travelling fairly fast.

Normally we would do between ten and fifteen miles a day, but in the more populated areas we could spend up to a week covering only twenty miles as the interviews John had with the local people were more numerous.

One evening while John was still busy, Matanda and I with one of the messengers decided to go and see if we could do a little hunting near the camp. We had seen some vultures in a tree so we went in that direction to investigate. As we drew near we saw a lioness lying along one of the bigger branches. This was enough for us, and we ran back to camp as quickly as we could to tell John what we had seen. Just then a moran came to say that a pride of five lion had been creating havoc with cattle in the area and could John help them by shooting them. Our trek that day had been a long one and John was feeling rather tired, but he promised to do what he could the next morning if the moran could establish exactly where the lion were located. The moran replied that they knew where they were: under the tree where we had seen the lioness. So John went off with his gun-bearer and one of the game scouts to see if he could find the pride. By the time he had reached the tree, however, they had moved off and as it was late he returned to camp.

During the night when we were asleep, the lion attacked the trek oxen, mauling one badly and scattering the rest. The uproar had everyone out of their beds and the rest of the night was spent in trying to round up the frightened cattle. Those that were found were put back into the enclosure, under guard, while the mauled beast was destroyed and put out as bait. Before dawn the lion returned to the kill and a large red-maned male was shot by the two game scouts who were watching over the bait.

This caused great excitement, and, had we not known the Masai, we should have thought it was the first lion they had ever seen. Hundreds of elders, morans, women and children turned up to look at the lion, and much abuse was hurled at the carcass. As we were to stay in the area for a few more days, Masai hospitality was lavished upon us. That night an ox was killed for our benefit and the next morning a fat sheep was produced, followed by another ox in the evening. We stayed there three nights and if John had not put his foot down and allowed only one beast to be slaughtered a day, the Masai would probably have killed three or four a day.

A few days later we arrived at a place called Seronera, heavily populated by the Masai. In this area the herds of cattle were small with very large flocks of sheep. These we learned were all on the move southward to the Moru Koppies. One of the big jobs to be done here was a stock census ordered by Central Government. Some of the flocks consisted of between five hundred and a thousand sheep and were being herded by youngsters not much older than Matanda and I. It was here that I first saw sheep grazing within fifty yards of lion, with neither taking any notice of the other.

The short rains now seemed to have started in earnest and we had from half-an-inch to an inch of rain regularly every afternoon. We spent about ten days at Seronera before going on to Moru where we saw large numbers of zebra, eland and wildebeest on the move because of the abundance of new green grass and water. These vast herds were followed up by prides of lion.

One evening John decided to entertain the camp by shooting a wildebeest, partially gutting it and towing it on a long chain pulled by four oxen. The carcass was dragged past a pride of lion, which started to eat it as it was being towed along and followed it right into the camp. Here another chain had been thrown over a tree and attached to a span of four more oxen. The first chain was unhitched and made fast to the one slung over the tree and the lion allowed to carry on eating quietly for a few minutes. When they were completely engrossed in their meal, the oxen were urged on to pull the chain; one lioness suddenly found herself hauled twenty feet into the air. This did not deter her, however, and she clung grimly to the carcass. The oxen were then pushed back and the wildebeest and lioness lowered to the ground. This performance was repeated two or three times; then the lions were left to finished their meal in peace. Matanda watched all this with wide eyes, then turned to me and said, 'Hey! Debbe! When we get circumcised we should come here to kill our lions!'

'Why come all this way?' I asked.

'Well, you can see the lion here are tame and stupid, like sheep, and easy to kill. But the Masai in our part don't know this - that there are two kinds of lion!'

The night, before we left for Moru, a report came in to the effect that the Masai had raided the Sukuma, a tribe that lived some fifty miles to the west of where we were camped. Three people had been killed, a number wounded and nearly three hundred head of cattle stolen. This was the first big Masai raid to occur since John had taken over as District Officer at Loliondo. He had already warned the morans that he would not tolerate this type of raid and that he would make it his personal duty to see the culprits caught and punished.

That night he called up all the senior members of his staff and instructed them where to go at Moru. He put Matanda and me in the charge of Saidi the cook and Martin the head drover. He told us we could only leave the camp accompanied by the two game scouts who were remaining with the main safari to protect the cattle. John picked out two policemen and his head messenger to go along with him and left later that night, telling us that he hoped to meet up with us in two or three days' time. Like Matanda he travelled light, carrying only a blanket, a water bottle and his gun.

We began our trek to Moru the next morning but did not reach there that night, sleeping out on the Plains. Up to this time we had been skirting the northern edge of the Serengeti, with scattered trees along our route. This day we left the last of the trees behind us during the morning and by noon were well out on to the Plains. Saidi was well prepared for this and the wagon was stacked with firewood.

Before reaching our camping place for that night we had to cross a small river. Normally it would have been dry - a sand-river - but now, owing to the rains, it was quite full. Unfortunately at this particular spot there were wide areas of black cotton soil on either side of the river. When we attempted to cross, the wheels of the wagon sank right up to the hubs. To make matters worse the oxen began to sink too. We struggled without success for half an hour before deciding to unload the wagon to lighten it. All the Sonjo were put to this task. I had only recently discovered that these men were not employees in the usual sense of the word, but were extra-mural prisoners working off their sentences. The other camp personnel that had gone ahead to set up camp were now called back to help us. Martin ordered that all the cattle were to be outspanned (unyoked), and then selected a completely fresh team, choosing the biggest and strongest oxen. The wagon was now fairly light and with the new team and everybody pushing as hard as they could, we eventually freed the wagon and got to the other side of the river.

The next morning was fine and dry. We had the usual visits from the local Masai, bringing gifts of milk and livestock. Martin and Saidi discussed the camp site, which they concluded was on too soggy ground and also too far from the main area of operations for John Pride. So the Sonjo were sent off with a messenger to prepare another camp.

The new site was in among tall fever trees, very attractive with their delicate leaves and yellow bark. It was a most pleasant place and we stayed there a full eight days. Late during our second night John returned with eight moran prisoners handcuffed together. They were in the charge of two ordinary policemen and four tribal askaris whom John had picked up on the way. These morans were later sent to Loliondo under guard where they, together with others who had taken part in the raid, were given sentences ranging from two years' imprisonment to the death penalty.

CHAPTER TEN

A WOMAN'S PLACE IN THE TRIBE

O N THE WAY TO MORU, Matanda had told me that he had heard there was to be a circumcision ceremony of girls at a Moru manyatta, at about the time we would be there. I asked him if we could go to see the ceremony, but he answered that layonis were not allowed to do so. However, he added, in spite of this he had in fact seen quite a few, and perhaps we could get to see this one - we would have to see how the land lay when we arrived. But when Matanda went to see some friends in one of the manyattas there, he came back with the news that the ceremony had already taken place. So we missed our chance of sneaking in among the calves to take a peep - which was how Matanda had got to see other circumcisions. It was just as well, as I would have been in serious trouble with John Pride had I been caught.

The Masai girl is treated, and behaves, in much the same way as the boy until she is old enough to carry out small chores. She then becomes an assistant to her mother, while the boy, as soon as he is old enough, goes out herding the livestock.

One of the girl's first duties is to gather up fresh cow dung to repair her mother's house. After a while the girl child is taught to split strips of olive wood for cleaning out calabashes, and to collect cows' urine for washing out the calabashes used for fresh milk. She also helps her mother milk the cows and later is taught how to assist in the building of a house, which is always a woman's job.

As soon as the girl begins to show an interest in boys, usually at about eight or nine years of age, she starts to go off with the layonis and practises sex play. So when she is ready to make love with the morans, aged about eleven to thirteen, she is no longer a virgin. If she decides she likes a particular moran more than the others, she asks his friends to invite him to drink milk with her on a certain day, in a ceremony called ngibot. She informs her mother she wants to have the ngibot, and some milk is set aside for two or three days beforehand. All the morans and nditos then dress up in beads and other finery, and smear themselves with red ochre before entering the manyatta. They eat the now curdled milk and dancing begins. An older ndito, who has already proved her worth to the morans, is then chosen to perform the ngibot ceremony. A calabash of milk, previously treated with olive ash, which makes it stay fresh for several days, is presented by her to the chosen moran and placed at his feet. When he has drunk all he can, he leads his new sweetheart to a hut, followed by the other young men and girls. They spend the night making love and are both now known as asanja.

A moran may have as many as fifty asanja at one time, and this applies to a girl too. An asanja always has priority over other girls, and a girl will remain the asanja of a moran until she marries. A situation can arise when a moran is so popular with the girls that he has a number of asanja in the same manyatta. This state of affairs sometimes leads to difficulties, so he is permitted to take his friends along to help him out. They all share one bed, which can take up to eight people, but each will remain with the same partner for the night, although they may change over the following night.

After an asanja association has been created, two further associations can evolve in the same ceremony. The first is the choosing of a girl known as oldipet. This girl becomes next in priority after the asanja. The second is known as olgiloti, where another girl – the third in line -is chosen. These two girls can change over their positions by mutual agreement, but the asanja retains her superior status until she joins her husband in marriage. This husband is very rarely the asanja moran I have just referred to. Sometimes a girl may marry her asanja, but this is not common, as her father has usually made prior marital arrangements for her, when she was still a small child.

When a moran visits a manyatta where he has an unmarried asanja, she will drop everything to spend her time with him - that is, of course, if she has not already made an arrangement for that day with one of her other asanja. What is so amazing about the asanja association is that there do not appear to be any jealousies, provided the rules of the game are adhered to.

After a girl's marriage she may still associate with her asanja, but he no longer has any special claim on her, and he now has to follow a different set of rules.

Marriage negotiations for a girl are often entered into between two fathers before she is actually born, and the bride price paid then too. If the baby is not a girl the arrangement can be carried on to the next pregnancy of the same wife or even to that of another wife of the same man. A girl, though bound to the husband her father chooses for her, does not become his wife in fact until after her circumcision when she will go to join him.

As soon as a girl starts to menstruate she is considered to be ready for circumcision. She herself has no say as to when it will take place as her mother will decide for her (except if she were to become pregnant, when, as mentioned above, she would be circumcised immediately) having consulted other mothers with daughters of approximately the same age. The matter is then discussed with the father who provides the wherewithal for the ceremony, which differs only in some details from that of a boy's circumcision.

The day before the girl's circumcision an olive sapling is planted by the men outside the manyatta as a sign. An ox is killed and split down the centre, the right side of the carcass being kept for the women, of which certain parts are reserved and prepared for use in fertility prayers. Any woman within sight of the slaughter is given a piece of meat, and this she must eat, as it would bring bad luck to refuse. The left side of the beast is for the men, and from it certain portions are removed and cooked separately for use in the re-naming ceremony, which is carried out by the men, for the circumcised girl will lose her name and be given a new one.

Early on the morning of the circumcision day the girl goes between her mother's hut and the fence enclosing the manyatta, and in this space bathes herself with water specially prepared as for a boy's circumcision. While she is doing this a hole is made in the roof to let in light for performing the operation, which is carried out by one of the older women. This woman is usually practised in the art, but it is not considered absolutely necessary. She must, however, undertake to complete the operation whatever happens. The girl is held down by a number of women and she can scream and fight as much as she likes, for there is no disgrace attached to this as there is with the boy's circumcision. But once the operation is started, it will be completed forcibly. There is no escape.

The circumcision consists of removing half an inch of skin around the clitoris, which itself is cut out to a depth of a quarter of an inch and a slash made below it towards the vagina. The reasons given for this crude and cruel operation are that it enlarges the vagina, thereby making childbirth easier; and that the removal of the clitoris will prevent sexual arousal, and therefore promiscuity.

After the circumcision is completed, the girl remains in her mother's hut for four months, during which time she is fed mainly on meat and fat. She is visited by both men and women, but no one may touch her bed except her mother, who is also the only one to prepare her food. Her betrothed is present on the day she is due to leave the hut, but first she is shaved, her hair having been allowed to grow during her confinement. Now every particle of body hair is removed. She is given back her beads and adornments, her mother helping her to look as beautiful as a bride should, and she is then presented to her husband.

During this first day it is the bride's responsibility to find out in which hut in the manyatta her husband is staying, so that when night falls she can go to join him. This little game goes on for several days while her father arranges for drink to be prepared. When the beer is ready everybody drinks his fill, and the elders bless the girl by spitting on her. Now finally she goes off with her husband to begin a new life.

On her arrival at her husband's manyatta she is taken to her mother-in-law's house where a party is already in progress. As soon as the sun goes down one of the prominent elders makes a speech, which is purely customary and part of the ritual. In it he tells the husband that he will be left alone on this night to enjoy his bride. He must thereafter never complain that he had not had the pleasure of sleeping with his wife for one night. The party disperses and the couple are left on their own. From now on the husband has the opportunity of sleeping with his wife only from time to time as he has to follow the Masai code of hospitality towards his own age-group and share his wife accordingly.

If her husband is not yet an elder the young wife may live with her mother-in-law for five or six years, depending on how well the two women get on with each other. Otherwise she may build her own house. All the work of constructing a house is done by women, and although it is known as the husband's house, the woman is in fact head of it.

When a traveller arrives at a manyatta he is greeted and, if his age-group is not known, he is asked what it is. He is then directed to a house belonging to a man of that age-group or, if there is no one in that category, to the house of a man in the next group-but-one up from his own - that is the group that lit the fire at his olpiron. Failing that, he goes to the house of one of the next group but one below him - the group whose fire he lit at their olpiron. In the event of there being only one house which he is qualified to enter in that manyatta, and if it is already occupied by other guests, he will double up with them, but the first guest to arrive is the one who will receive priority.

When a guest enters, the husband, if he is present, will sit and talk to the visitor and, after eating, will leave to seek other accommodation, allowing the guest to remain with his wife for the night. It is entirely up to the wife whether she wants the guest to share her bed or not. If she does, she will invite him to her bed; if she does not want him, she will tell him so and that is the end of the matter. Should there happen to be two guests, although this is not usual, they will share the large bed, even if one of them is her particular lover. It is taboo for a married woman to show preference for one guest over another.

Any children born to a woman are always those of her husband, irrespective of whether the natural father is known or not. There is one exception to this. If a woman married to a witch-doctor is expecting a child that is not his, the Masai say, it will be stillborn, having been bewitched in the womb. However, should it be born alive and the witch-doctor disclaims it, the baby will be laid in the gateway to the manyatta and the cattle driven through the gate as fast as possible. If there has been a mistake - and the child is in fact that of the witch-doctor - it will survive, emerging from the ordeal untouched. However, for a witch-doctor to disclaim a child is very rare, whether it is his or not.

When a woman has produced her fourth child a special ceremony is held. An ox is killed, beer is prepared and, as a sign of respect, she is given a new name. She can now use either of her two names as she pleases. Her first two sons are given these names in the order of their birth, and the third son is given his father's name. When she reaches the menopause, providing she has had four or more children, she is given the freedom of the manyatta, for she has carried out her duty as a mother successfully. She is presented with a large sheepskin cloak with a white border, which she wears without jewellry or leg- and arm-wires. She no longer has to do any work and enjoys the same status as a male elder. These privileges remain hers for the rest of her life.

On the other hand, should a woman be barren, she would not gain any real respect from the manyatta, and her husband could return her to her parents and claim back part of the bride-price, although he does not necessarily get it.

On the death of a woman, her sons anoint her body with sheep fat. She is taken from the manyatta and carried some distance to be laid under a tree. A piece of animal skin is tied to a branch above so that it hangs down just over her eyes to prevent them being picked out by vultures. During the night hyenas come and devour the body.

The same custom applies to a man, except that in his case his head is laid on a green trunk cut from a particular tree. His son then makes a request of his dead father to protect him in his immature life and to let him die of old age.

If a Masai dies inside a hut, it is the custom to call in the corpse carriers to remove the body, and this requires the payment of one ox. In order to avoid paying this fee, dying people are sometimes put out for the hyenas by their families before actual death, but the dying person must be in such a condition that death is obviously inevitable within one full day.

CHAPTER ELEVEN

THE LAIBON'S STORY

*W*E WERE NOW HAVING RAIN fairly regularly every day. It usually started between four and five o'clock in the afternoon and continued until the early hours of the morning. This made camp life at Moru rather difficult at night, but during the day we had mainly sunny weather. This gave Matanda and me ample opportunities to roam the area, always accompanied by the game scouts of course.

We frequently met prides of lion of up to twenty animals or more. For some reason they did not bother about us at all. It may have been because few of them had been shot at, and they were used to living at close quarters with the Masai and were therefore accustomed to the smell of human beings. Also there was abundant game in the area, and a lion had to exert itself very little to obtain food. Sometimes we would walk to within thirty yards of a pride and not see them until we were almost upon them. I should not care to do this today, having had experiences with more aggressive lion outside the Serengeti.

One afternoon we had a very heavy thunderstorm, and a large fever tree some distance from the camp was struck by lightning and collapsed. A loud scuffle and the roar of a lion followed this event. John Pride jumped to his feet and, picking up his rifle as he ran past his tent, called to the game scouts to follow him. We heard two shots and John shouted that we could go to see what had happened. One lion had been killed by the lightning and another paralysed. This was a female, and John had quickly put the poor creature out of her misery with clean shots through her brain.

After the thunder there was a short, heavy shower and the night that followed was beautiful, starlit and clear. Unfortunately, the lioness that had been destroyed must have been on heat, as the remaining males of other prides were drawn to the camp and prowled around all night, coming so close at one point that a game scout was forced to shoot one of them. The trek oxen were in a great state of agitation over the presence of the lion and everyone stayed awake to keep the cattle under control.

Early the next morning John sent out messengers to inform the Masai that all further interviews would have to be held at Lion Hill, eight miles away. He decided on this sudden move, as it was obvious that our gang of very tired men would have difficulty keeping the oxen quiet if the events of the previous night were repeated. We moved out at nine o'clock, leaving behind the lion that were still keeping watch over the area and becoming more and more bad tempered. For a short while this experience at Moru made Matanda and me, and most of the others, show a far greater respect for lion. But, as familiarity breeds contempt, it was not long before we were once again regarding them as large cats.

The trek from Moru to Lion Hill was one that will always remain in my memory. For the first time I saw the full migration of wildebeest across the Serengeti Plains, an unforgettable sight. It was difficult to judge the numbers, but from Moru Koppies one could see for a radius of ten miles, and the whole area was solid with animals all moving at a fast grazing pace towards the east.

Two or three years later we went to watch the migration coming through the Ngurumeti bottleneck, a gap between the river and the hills which, at the spot above where we stood, was less than two hundred yards wide. Here the animals were travelling as fast as they could past the obstructions of other, slower animals in their path. Just prior to our arriving there, poachers had been active and carcasses lay strewn on all sides. Predators were also much in evidence, but for the two hours we watched the game going through the gap no actual kills were made, for the predators had by that time gorged themselves.

An advance party of the Sonjo extra-mural prisoners had been sent to set up camp, so when we arrived we found it ready. I was pleased because I also found my parents waiting for us, together with the Veterinary Officer. They had brought a lorry-load of stores for our safari and they spent the night at the camp before leaving for home the next day. I never for a moment questioned their arrival, nor how they had located us in that vastness. In Africa these things just happen. News travels fast and no doubt some young moran, standing relaxed on one leg in the middle of nowhere, had been asked where we were and had told them.

That night one of the lesser Masai witch-doctors stopped at our camp on his way to Moru. John asked him to join us at the fire, for the purpose of obtaining information of the area. This was his usual practise when meeting someone he thought might be of use to him; and the visitor would be settled beside the fire, given food and a few large brandies and encouraged to talk, although at that time it was illegal to give spirits to the Masai. The guest would begin to tell stories and, apart from the useful information that was often allowed to slip out, John loved to hear about the Masai customs and beliefs. On this particular night, for the benefit of those present, John asked the laibon to tell us how the institution of marriage came about amongst the Masai people, and the witch-doctor related this legend.

In the long, long ago, the Masai never married, but lived in family groups and, as incest was the usual practise, the members of the group were closely related to one another. To one of those groups came a time of great famine and they realised that unless they could move their stock to country where there was grazing and water, they would perish. In this group was a moran, his brother, who was an elder layoni, and their sister - a particularly attractive young ndito. The rest of the group were either old or incapable of physical labour. So the elder called all the family together, and, at this meeting, told the moran that he, his brother and sister were to take the cattle to find a new land with sweet grass and flowing water. Before they left, the elder said they must slaughter two oxen. The meat of these animals was to be dried and left behind to sustain the family that remained. The meat was duly dried and the fat rendered down. Having done this, the moran, the layoni and the ndito left with all the stock.

After travelling for eight days, they came upon an area of lush grass and plentiful water, and here the moran decided to stay. They set up a temporary manyatta consisting of a thorn-bush enclosure for the cattle and a hut for themselves.

The girl's job was to sew loin-cloths from calf-skin and to prepare food but, as the brothers thought it unwise to leave her unprotected all day alone in a strange country, they made a hole in the ground for her to stay in while they were out herding the cattle. They placed a log across the hole; lying from north to south, and allowing light to fall on her sewing from the east in the morning and from the west in the evening. As the day advanced and the sun passed over, she would turn gradually with the light.

One day while the ndito was in the hole, eight strange warriors appeared. As they were tired they sat upon the log-and blocked out the light. She waited for a time for them to move but soon lost patience and stuck her needle into the bottom of one of the warriors. He jumped up saying, 'There's a scorpion here! Lift up the log and kill it.' They raised the log and, to their wonder, found the beautiful young girl sitting in the hole. When she saw them she became very frightened, but they assured her that all they wanted was drink, and her favours. After giving them water, she took them, one at a time, into the hut where they made love to her. They stayed on for a while and talked to the girl. She had taken a fancy to these strange warriors and asked them to come again. This they promised to do, and they returned the next day. After this their visits became a regular daily occurrence.

One day, when the layoni came home with the calves he happened to notice that there were ten spear holes outside the hut, and over the next three or four days he made a point of checking on this. Every morning there were two spear holes, and in the evening there were ten. He mentioned this strange phenomenon to his brother and, after talking the matter over, they decided that on the next day they would go out as usual, but then the layoni would return quietly and hide himself among the youngest calves, that were left in the boma. As his loin-cloth was made of calf-skin, he would not be noticed.

The strangers arrived and as was now their custom let the ndito out of the hole and made love to her. This day, however, for the first time, they suggested to her that they should kill her brothers and take her and all the cattle to their manyatta. By this time the girl was in love with them all and ready to agree to anything they said as long as she could stay with them. She warned the warriors that her brothers were very strong and fierce, and had both killed lions and three men single-handed, so they should be very careful. She then laid down a plan of action.

'When my men come home in the evening,' she said, 'they are usually tired but have still to do the milking. By the time they come to milk the last cow, which has a lot of milk but is very fierce, they are exhausted. They have to tie this cow up to be able to milk her, so you should hide in the boma behind the hut. When you hear the moran tell the layoni to bring the rope to tie the cow, then is the time to pounce on them. They will have no weapons and will be powerless.'

The layoni heard his sister's plan to kill his brother and him, and repeated every word to the moran when he brought the cattle home in the evening. So instead of doing the milking and becoming worn out, they made a counter-plan. The moran pretended to be extra tired that day, and said he had been obliged to go further than usual for grazing. Playing for time, he and his brother made a show of doing the milking until it got dark. The moran then shouted for the rope and quickly moved away from the fierce cow to join the layoni who, in the meanwhile, had collected their weapons. On hearing the call for the rope, the strangers pounced and thrust their spears, mistakenly, into the cow. With that the brothers appeared, fully armed, and killed them.

The next day they abandoned their temporary manyatta and began the long journey home, where they found the rains had started. On their arrival the two brothers called a meeting, which was attended by a number of families, and told their story. After a great deal of consideration, it was decided that the Masai should sell all their daughters as the girls were so unreliable and obviously preferred strangers. In their place they would buy in girls from other tribes (meaning other clans); the very fact that they were owned by the men would, the elders felt, engender feelings of respect in the purchased females. 'And this,' concluded the laibon, 'was how marriage began amongst the Masai.'

We woke to a cloudburst the next morning, which continued until well after midday. John, therefore, decided to wait at Lion Hill for the weather to improve; however, it continued to rain heavily and we were there for a further four nights before deciding to go on to Olduvai, it not being practical to delay any longer. Unfortunately the incessant rain had caused the soil to become absolutely sodden and the wagon was inevitably and repeatedly bogged down. At one stage we had twenty-six oxen inspanned with no load on the wagon, and yet, at the end of the day, with everyone aching and exhausted, we had only covered a distance of some five miles.

That night we slept on the treeless Plains. The only firewood we had was that what we had brought with us. However, it was not sufficient, for there had been a change in the weather, and although there was with no rain, it had turned bitterly cold. By now the main migration had arrived in the place, and the stretch between Lion Hill and Olduvai was a seething mass of wildebeest, zebra, eland, kongoni and Grant's and Thomson's gazelle. There were a few prides of lion and, scattered amongst the plains game, some hyena and cheetah.

At about noon on the fourth day after leaving Lion Hill, we arrived on the edge of the Olduvai Gorge. We had seen no human habitation along the last stretch until we reached here, where there were several Masai manyattas. We were told by a local Masai that there was a group of Europeans in the Gorge to the west, doing some excavations. These turned out to be Dr L. S. B. Leakey and his party of archeo-paeleontologists, on one of their early trips to the

Gorge. This culminated in his discovery of a number of important hominid fossils, which he stored with my parents at Loliondo for some time (no elaboration on Mary or Louis Leakey's findings is needed here, as these are now well-known throughout the world).

Over the next three days we made short moves along the northern edge of the Gorge, until we found a place where it petered out and where we crossed the Olduvai River. The following day we arrived at Olbalbal on the north-western slope of the Ngorongoro Crater, which was the most populated part we had so far visited. There were no less than seventeen manyattas in a tract of twenty square miles, and to deal with the problems brought to him by the Masai, took John and his staff a full two days. After this he was free to reconnoitre a track down into the crater; and he set off with a few of the Nandi, who could judge the best trail for the cattle to follow, and a couple of Masai as guides.

They were back very late but believed that they had found a suitable way down. John gave Martin, the head drover, instructions to take the next day all the Sonjo prisoners, and as many other people as he could find, to make a start on preparing the track, which had been marked out. This arduous task took two days to complete, and on the morning of the third we were ready to begin the descent into the crater.

On the rim of this natural wonder we halted. It is an incomparable sight, over eleven miles from one side to the other, the floor quite flat and the bowl almost symmetrical with walls up to two thousand feet high. Here we took everything off the wagon; the baggage already tied into conveniently sized bundles for carrying as head-loads. The prisoners acted as porters and set off down the track with the heaviest loads on their first trip, returning later for the lighter ones.

Next came the operation of getting the wagon down. Arap Maina, a burly six-foot Nandi, was chosen for the job of brake-man, and for the first time during the whole journey a man was put out in front to guide the oxen. John himself went ahead and called for the wagon to follow. The descent was done in short stretches of about a hundred yards at a time, so progress was slow but careful and there were no mishaps. By four o'clock the wagon was down and parked beside the baggage. It was reloaded and a fresh team of oxen inspanned. Despite the slow pace of the move, the team that had brought the wagon down were very fatigued, particularly the two rear animals. The oxen were watered and then allowed to follow us at their own pace as we moved on. In six hours we had covered six miles and dropped some thousand feet down what was nothing more than a game track. I wondered, having got down, how we would ever get up again, but Martin thought this would not be as difficult as the descent, provided the wagon was empty. As it turned out, he was right.

We were to camp that night near a koppie about five miles away in the south-west corner of the crater, above which stands today, high on the rim, a game lodge and a hotel. Some of the Sonjo had gone on ahead and when we arrived at nightfall we found the ever-hospitable Masai already there, an ox slaughtered, cut up and roasting on a fire. The Masai do not, as is commonly believed, just hack a carcass into chunks. Each piece is most carefully removed from the animal, having been cut a certain way for its own particular method of cooking. Every portion is specially allocated to individuals, depending on their seniority as guests or members of a family, and also for particular reasons of the health, age, childbearing state of the eater, or for special occasions. There are some hundred different cuts of meat in all.

The crater was teeming with game and Matanda and I spent three wonderful days hunting eland, zebra and wildebeest along the Ngare Nanyuki River. But we had now reached the end of our safari, and after eight days in the crater it was time to start back on the long trek to Loliondo via Olbalbal and the eastern edge of the Serengeti to Malambo, now known as Olaalaa. We had lost six trek oxen on the trip, but as we had brought three complete teams, we still had plenty of pulling power. Apart from the ascent up the crater wall, where we increased the number of animals on the wagon to twenty-four, we had no real difficulties on the way to Malambo. Water was plentiful, grazing was good throughout, and the rains were now easing off.

On our arrival at Malambo we were just in time for the start of the annual cattle market arranged by the Administration, chiefly for the purpose of collecting taxes. Most of the buyers came from Kenya, mainly Somalis with a sprinkling of Arabs. Accompanying these cattle traders were travelling hawkers, their wares transported on the backs of donkeys. Some of them would have anything up to a hundred and twenty donkeys, and the bulk of their trade consisted of bartering beads, red ochre, maize meal, salt, steel and brass wire, and trinkets in exchange for hides. However, a lot of purchases would be for cash and some of the bigger caravans would stay in the area buying up hides, sheep and goats until they had exhausted their supply of ready money.

Normally there was only one market held each year at Malambo, and this was the one we witnessed; but in years of famine the Administration would organise an extra market, usually in July, at which the Masai could sell their cattle and buy in food. At these sales the price of stock was invariably very low, not only because of the poor quality of the cattle - which had trekked long distances without regular watering points and sufficient grazing - but also because of the large numbers of animals on offer.

Usually three or four days elapsed before the bulk of the purchases were made, as the Masai would sell half a dozen animals then close the gate of the market with an olive branch while they held a meeting to discuss the price structure. Several hours later they would ask the auctioneer to start selling again. This procedure would be repeated a number of times and, although the reason given for this was that the Masai felt themselves to be done down, I am quite convinced it was a sport for the elders, similar to the morans' cattle-stealing. During the period of haggling the elders had absolutely nothing to do except drink, and eat the animals slaughtered and prepared for them by the morans.

We spent a week at Malambo and then left for Loliondo. Travelling from here on was good and John was keen to get back. Thirteen days later we arrived home having had but one mishap. Outside Soitai-ayo we were raided by lion and lost three head of cattle. We sat up over one of the kills that night and a game scout killed a lion while John wounded another. This meant we could not leave the area until the wounded animal had been found. Two of the game scouts followed the tracks and the search very nearly ended in tragedy. Luckily, however, they were together and when the lion attacked one man, who had missed with his first shot; the other game scout fired and killed it as it was about to maul him. He suffered no damage other than a couple of bruises and superficial scratches.

CHAPTER TWELVE

MASAI LEGENDS

*I*HAD AT FIRST FAVOURED THE IDEA of going to school, but when I learnt that I was not to have the freedom I had had in the past, and also that Matanda could not go with me, my heart sank. It was explained to me that white boys had to go to school and that I could always have a good life in the holidays, so in time I accepted the decision. At this stage I was ten and a half and could not write my name. I suppose my mother could have given me lessons, but she was always extremely busy and had few moments to herself.

On arriving at Ngaramtoni near Arusha, I was taken to a family called Boshoff, with whom I was to live. The school was less than a quarter of a mile from their farm and consisted of one large grass-thatched classroom with a small office and store at the far end. The walls were mud and wattle and only three feet high, except for the office and store, so the school could not in any way be termed comfortable, especially when the wind blew through from end to end. Added to this was the fact that the desks were made from old petrol boxes.

There were, at the time I started, eighteen children. I was the nineteenth, and they were all Afrikaners with the exception of a brother and sister who were English, like me. For three days after my arrival I did nothing but cry, but eventually I got over it and made friends with the schoolmaster's son. There were only three forms - Standards I, II and III - and the master, Mr van Wyk, taught all subjects and all classes.

I did not go home for the holidays; at the beginning of the next term I was put into Standard II, purely on account of my age, as I was by far the most backward child in the school. However, during the holidays I had done a considerable amount of work under the direction of Mr Boshoff's daughter, and at the end of this term - my first full one - which was also the annual examination term, I managed somehow to come top of the class. The day after the results were known my parents picked me up to take me home for the holidays at Loliondo; and this was the end of my schooling for some time. Things were going extremely badly on the farm and with our shops, and my parents could not afford to send me back. Once I had settled down again to the routine of life at Loliondo, I did not fancy the idea of ever returning to school anyhow, so this suited me to perfection.

In Loliondo at this time there were three shops: ours and two belonging to Asians who had bought out the previous owners. Past the last shop, on the road out of Loliondo, we had a hundred-and-fifty acres of maize field. One evening while John Pride, Drag Cartnell, the Veterinary Officer, and my parents were in conversation together, my stepfather mentioned how amazing it was that the field nearest to habitation should have suffered the most damage by game, and he wondered if some of the game was not perhaps two-legged. John remarked that all game was grey in the dark, and if anyone got hurt it would be their own fault.

A few days later my stepfather was seen removing pellets from twelve-bore shot-gun ammunition and replacing them with salt crystals. When asked what was the idea, all he would say was, 'You'll see in due course.'

That evening he called for our watchmen on this particular field and told them there was to be a big drive to rid the maize of game once and for all. Everybody should accompany him and the head watchmen for posting at strategic points, as soon as it got dark. I asked if I could go too, but was told firmly that I could not. The men were lectured about being careful with one another, and my stepfather made it clear that no one was to use a spear or bow and arrows against anything, unless and until he gave the command.

At about eight o'clock everyone congregated at the main maize store and from there were sent to their posts. An hour and a half later two shots were heard, followed by shouts, screams and yells and the sound of a lorry moving off. My stepfather left the field soon after this, saying he thought a man had been wounded but obviously not seriously as all that had been left behind was blood and some bits of material. Whoever it was, he said, must have been well organised, as there had been a number of people to help, in addition to having a lorry to cart the maize away. As there were only two people with lorries in Loliondo, other than our own and those belonging to the Government, it was quite obvious who the people concerned were. This was easy to narrow down further, as one of the two had no facilities for milling maize and would have found it too expensive to move it all the way to the nearest mill at Narok. So by simple deduction, there could be but one particular culprit.

I think my stepfather had known all along who was stealing the maize, and so had the District Officer. However, nothing more was said about the matter until the next morning when they walked together into one of the shops and asked to see the owner. His wife said she was very sorry, but her husband had gone to Narok. John Pride enquired how he had got there as the only transport were the two lorries, both of which were still in Loliondo at that moment. At this she became very flustered and said her husband had walked. The occupants of the shop, including one or two African shoppers, all burst into laughter, as they knew the shop-keeper was incapable of walking one mile, let alone a hundred and ten.

John thanked the wife and he and my stepfather left. Outside they discussed the situation and the District Officer said he would have to issue a search warrant in case the man was there and perhaps badly wounded, in which event he would have to be taken to Loliondo to avoid any unpleasant repercussions. He returned later with a couple of police constables and the husband was found in bed complete with a peppering of salt crystals, mainly in his backside but extending up as far as his neck.

John brought the news of this painful state of affairs to our house, adding that the man would be immobile for a few days and that he had admitted responsibility for the thefts of maize. 'What's more,' he went on, 'our thief is prepared to waive any action against you, provided you don't take any against him!'

I pointed out that he hadn't a leg to stand on, and that even if he died it would be nobody's fault but his own. This, however, was very unlikely.

The other shopkeeper was delighted, and said it was the best news he had heard in a long time. He celebrated with a party at his shop a few days later and invited everyone of importance, including the injured man who unfortunately could not attend.

The outcome of this little incident was that no action was taken on either side and the matter was treated as a huge joke. The man recovered and became a great admirer of my stepfather, acquiring as a natural consequence the nickname of Chumvi (salt) amongst the local population.

The Masai, as with most tribes, enjoy little scandals like this, taking great delight in passing them on to others, and round the cooking fires they are keen story-tellers, one tale blending into the next with no real beginnings or endings. Animals and insects play a natural part in the ancient tribal memories, and it seemed to me, listening wide-eyed as a boy, that the Masai could find an explanation for everything. Our bellies full of good roasted meat and bodies reeking of wood-smoke, Matanda and I would nudge and pester the morans to tell us a story. And perhaps one would stretch his legs towards the fire and say, 'Long, long ago, when all animals and humans were equal . ...' 'Really?' we would ask, and he would reply that this was a fact. All spoke the same language and shared everything alike. The humans ate bark and roots, while some of the animals did the same. Other animals grazed on grass and young shoots. There was great happiness and no quarrelling, until one day the rhino, which always went to water in the middle of the day in the hot sun, found that if he lay down in the pool he felt cooler and more comfortable. But this muddied the water and made it undrinkable for the others, so the human asked the rhino to stop dirtying the pool, but he took no notice.

On the third occasion that the human complained, the rhino said, 'You are too small and insignificant to order me about. I shall do as I please!'

The human went off and found some iron, ore which he beat into a sharp instrument, and with this he returned to the waterhole. The rhino was rolling about in ecstasy in the mud and was caught unawares when the human jumped on his back and stuck the sharpened tool into his tough hide, piercing his heart and killing him.

The rhino missing, the human explained what had happened. Together with all the animals and humans, God strode to the pool and called to the rhino to get up and live. He instructed the rhino to behave with love towards his fellow creatures and to remember that they had all to live in peace together. Although he was a big animal, God told him, it did not give him the right, as they had witnessed, to menace others.

Shortly after this, man's woman had a child and the bull's cow had a calf; but the woman had no milk for her child and it cried continuously and lost weight. The calf, however, grew big and frisky and the cow's udder leaked milk, so the man went to the bull and said, 'Look, Bull, your cow's calf is healthy and fat and yet your cow, who has four teats while my woman has only two, is leaking milk on to the earth. My child is starving while yours is thriving. You heard what God said: we must all live happily together and help one another.'

So the bull told his cow to reserve two teats for the use of the man's child. She said she would allow the child to suckle one teat and, together with its own mother's two, would give it nourishment from three. As the child was smaller than the calf, this was adjudged fair, and in due course the child grew in size and was healthy. The humans increased and the cattle too, but in even greater numbers.

One day one of the human children fell ill and when it recovered it was thin and weak. In order to build up its strength it had to have fat, so the mother went to one of the cows and said, 'You have a lot of fat in your milk which my child needs, but it cannot drink enough milk to get sufficient fat. What am I to do?'

The cow replied, 'Find a calabash, dry it, break the top and remove all the pith and seeds. You will then have a container to hold liquid. When you have done this, bring it to me.'

The mother did as she was instructed, and when she returned the cow allowed her milk to flow into the calabash until it was full. 'Now take it', the cow said, 'and put it in the shade. When it goes sour the fat will rise to the surface. Skim this off and feed it to your child and drink the rest yourself. This will help you to improve your milk flow.'

Soon the child recovered; and some time later the father went to the bull and asked for some partly digested grass for medicinal purposes, as his woman had not conceived again. The bull told him to wait until he had grazed enough grass and was resting, chewing the cud. The man was then to hold the bull's tongue and pull it. This would make him sick and bring up the cud.

Man's next request, for marrow from the shin-bone of the bull, was too much, and the bull turned to him in anger and said, 'I now realise that all you want to do is kill me. We have lived in harmony so long. My cows have helped to rear your children, and when they were sick my cows produced fat for them. When your woman was barren I gave her cud. But if you must kill me, do it the right way. Go and fetch your sharpened instrument with which you killed the rhino and follow my tail all the length of my back until you reach my neck. Where my neck ends and my head begins you will find a hollow. Stick your tool into this and I shall die. But from today our friendship ends. I will serve you as a servant but you will have to work for everything I give you.

'Firstly, I shall no longer drop my dung in one place, but will scatter it, so that when your woman builds her house she will have to go about and pick up my dung, and carry it from many different places. Secondly, you will have to milk my cows by hand, and you will have to catch them and tie them up. You will be able to milk them only in the early morning and the late evening, and you will have to sing to them with a sweet voice to make them let down their milk. Thirdly, when we cattle go out grazing we will not go alone, and if we do we will not return. In future you will have to accompany us wherever we go and carry a stick with which to hit us to make us do what you want. Nor will we defend ourselves against other animals, and you will have to build a boma in which to keep us, driving us in at night and out again in the morning.'

So the bull was killed and all was as he said it would be. From that day on the cattle and goats went with the Masai, and the game animals - he eland, the wildebeest, the buffalo and all the others - went with the Oldorobo.

One day the Oldorobo woman slaughtered an eland just as the herd was going out to graze. When her son was called to accompany them, the woman refused to let him go until he had eaten some liver from the dead eland. So the herd went out alone and, after he had eaten, the son went to look for them. By that time they had wandered too far, and when he did eventually find them the rains had come; the grazing was good and the eland refused to go back to the dry country that the Oldorobo roamed. So, in order to live, the Oldorobo had to work for the Masai.

One evening, a very attractive Oldorobo maiden, tired after working all day, and just about to rest, was ordered to fetch water from a river a long way off while her Masai friends flirted and made love. The next day she called a meeting of the Oldorobo women, and they agreed to tell their men that they were no longer prepared to slave for the Masai. But the men said they had no choice as there was nothing for them to live on, now that they had lost their herds of eland. The girl said, 'Nonsense! The animals are still ours, grazing on good lush grass. We will follow them and live with them. When we are hungry we can kill an eland and eat it where it falls.' So the men agreed and the Oldorobo have lived in this way ever since.

In those days a big liana rope came down from heaven where God lived. He was called Ngai, and his rope was called Ngenengai. One day a dog, breathing heavily, came down the rope and was seen by a Masai lying under a tree.

'Lenanu', he called, using the old name for a dog, 'why are you breathing like that'?

'Because I have eaten a sheep,' Lenanu replied. 'It had a large tail and was very fat, and its meat was tender and cool. You should try eating a sheep.'

So the Masai went up the rope and when he met God, God asked him why he had come and the Masai told him, 'To ask you for a sheep.'

God said, 'How do you know about such a creature as a sheep?'

So the Masai answered, 'Lenanu told me.'

God sent for the dog and asked him why he had given away a secret, when he had been told not to. 'For your punishment you will now become a scavenger, eating left-over food and human excreta; and you will no longer be called Lenanu, but Ndia.'

'In that case,' Ndia said, 'will you please turn my heart so I am not sick when I eat bad things, and make my sense of smell keen so that I can pick up the odour of left-over food more easily. Also my hair must be turned backwards in order not to get caught up in the bush when I am scavenging and to make it easier for me to run away if I am found stealing. Will you improve my speed too, so I can run as fast as a gazelle.'

All this God agreed to, and the Masai was then given sheep. Ever since, sheep have remained the special property of the Masai tribe, and no one else has a right to possess them unless the Masai have given their permission.

The Oldorobo were jealous when they heard of God's gift to the Masai and went to the Masai and said, 'You have used us unscrupulously in the past and we are now going to cut your liana so you can no longer climb up to God with your requests.' And this they did, and, from that day on, the Masai people have been out of direct contact with God.

A little later the Masai, the dog, the bee and the fly decided that as they were all in close association, a decision should be made as to who should inherit the property of the Masai when he died. At this meeting the fly was the first to speak. He claimed he should inherit as he always accompanied the human and his stock wherever they went-whether out grazing, or in the hut, or at milking.

The dog claimed that he too went everywhere with the human, warning him of danger and protecting the cattle, and no matter what the weather, always sleeping out of doors. He had to fight the jackal and hyena who would take a newborn calf from its mother-but he, the dog, would only eat the afterbirth which otherwise would rot and smell in the manyatta.

Then came the turn of the bee who said he was descended from the maggot in the cow's dung and was therefore very closely associated with the Masai's most valued belonging, the cow. This, said the bee, cannot be doubted. Besides, he had to collect nectar for the man and fight battles to protect the honey. He had only one arrow, and when it had been thrown he would die. All this the bee had to do for the Masai who needed the honey for making beer so that he could acquire a bride and increase the Masai population. Without honey, the bee stated, the Masai cannot marry and would therefore die out as a race. For his endeavours the bee received no return, and for that reason, not only his property, but the Masai himself should belong to the bee.

The Masai was then asked if he had anything to say. 'Yes,' he said, 'in my opinion the dog, who apart from everything else gave me the secret of the sheep, should inherit my property.' But the bee and the fly disagreed with this and in the end it was decided that the bee had truly the strongest claim. Since then the bee has owned the Masai, who is also related to the bee.

CHAPTER THIRTEEN

WILD DOGS & PORCUPINES

*T*HE STRONG AFFINITY BETWEEN THE BEE and the Masai in their legends was not always much in evidence when they came in contact with an angry swarm.

The Masai love of honey is intense, and they will go almost to any lengths to procure it, provided they can get an Oldorobo or one of the associated tribesmen to do the actual work of extracting the honey from the hive. Few morans will brave the dangers of being stung, or of falling from a tree and breaking their necks. As it would be no disgrace for a layoni to be hurt or even killed in the attempt, those who were not particularly susceptible to bee stings would invariably have a go if they found a hive.

Matanda and I were down at the river bathing in a small pool, which we had made by damming up the water with a wall of stones and mud. We had set our bird traps and were just waiting for them to be filled. This usually took about an hour, after which we would find a catch of somewhere between two and six birds. The traps were made with wildebeest-tail hair wound into a noose and tied to a piece of string. The noose was about three inches in diameter and each piece of string held a dozen or so, depending on the size of the waterhole or patch of food which the birds would go for. Waterholes were generally the best places, but only effective in the very dry seasons when the rivers were not running.

A bird would push its head through the noose to get to the water, and the noose would tighten, the bird fluttering about until it killed itself by strangulation.

While we were there three layonis appeared and asked us what we were doing. Matanda by this time quite enjoyed washing and splashing about in water, though he was not over-enthusiastic about soap, claiming it was not he who was against it but that the cattle in the boma, and his mother did not like the smell. We told the layonis we were bathing and invited them to join us. One seemed keen but the other two said, 'Don't cut the branch you're sitting on,' (don't be a fool) and that they would prefer to go honey-hunting: they had just heard a honey-bird up river. This seemed a good idea, so Matanda and I quickly got dressed and went with them.

The honey-bird directs humans by calling and jumping from tree to tree, leading them to food of any sort. This is usually honey but can often be a wild animal such as a rhinoceros or even a large snake. After the human has taken what he wants of either the honey or the kill, the honey-bird will pick up what is left, such as congealed blood, bees' wax or young, undeveloped bees in the comb. So when following a honey-bird you have to be particularly careful as you could very easily be led into danger. The Masai have often used this bird to uncover cattle thefts when they suspect there is an olpul of stolen cattle in a certain area.

The five of us spread out, all shouting 'Aaagh, aaagh!' and knocking two bits of wood together and whistling from time to time, until we found the bird and followed it as it hopped from tree to tree making its peculiar call of 'Chweeti-chwee-ti' while we called back to it. Our progress was very slow as the honey-bird does not follow a straight line, but after about an hour it eventually settled in a big cedar tree.

The tree was surrounded by thick bush, which covered the best part of a quarter of an acre. We knew that whatever it was the bird had led us to was either in the tree or in the bush at its base: we had come to the tricky part, which can be quite dangerous. We regretted not having the dogs with us that day as they were generally very good about giving fair warning of danger.

After circling the bushes three or four times, we got a bit braver and started to lob stones in, and so gradually came up to the trunk of the tree. There, about thirty-five feet up, one of the layonis spotted bees going in and out of an opening in the trunk. We lit a small fire and Matanda went off to fetch an axe as it was obvious that we were not going to enlarge the hole with our knives. Meanwhile one of the other boys collected moss off adjoining trees and the rest of us cut a couple of forked sticks to use as a ladder, as there were no branches for the first twenty feet.

A layoni now attempted to climb the tree but one of the forked sticks slipped, and with all the shouting the bees' attention was attracted and we were suddenly and fiercely attacked. This is usually a good sign, as bees that are quiet or calm normally have very little honey. Eventually Matanda suggested that we put out the fire so as not to attract anyone, and return later when it was dark and the bees quieter. So we hid the axe and arranged to meet at sundown.

That night, helped by smoke from burning moss and an improved ladder, we were able to extract a considerable amount of beautiful white honey and a lot of combs containing the young bees still in the milky stage, quantities of which we consumed on the spot. It was the first time I had eaten young bees, which are like tiny maggots to look at, white and pus-like. I must admit I did not enjoy the taste much, but I was not prepared to let the side down by saying so. To the Masai they are a delicacy.

After we had collected up all the honey, we had over four gallons. This we shared between us, a bigger portion going to me as I did

A junior Moran from a warrior manyatta.

A Masai bride. Sha has been completely shaved and her mother has helped her to dress up in all her finery and ornaments before she is presented to the husband her father has chosen for her.

A Masai home. These huts, constructed entirely by the women, are made of fine twigs covered with a light layer of grass or leafed branches and plastered with cow dung.

A Masai hut under repair; the women is about to plaster on fresh cow dung to fill in the cracks.

Asanja calabashes. An Ndito will present milk in one of these to her chosen Asanja (sweetheart). They are decorated with beads and cowrie shells – the shells are a Masai fertility symbol.

Unafraid; a Layoni protecting his flock from lions at Moru Koppies, Serengeti.

Young David Read with one of his lion cubs and a puppy at Wasonyiro, 1929. (Note the model 'T' Ford in the background).

Treed by Wild dogs (African Hunting dogs). David takes to a tree to escape a pack of Wild Dogs – the most savage and voracious of African Cooperative predators.

Above: Oldimbau, a Masai Laigwanan, last of the hereditary chiefs in Tanzania. He met Princess Margaret in 1957.

Below: David's mother (left) and step-father, Otto Fischer (right), after their vehicle broke down in Masailand (1930).

A married Masai women in all her finery. The coiled disks show that she has sons who are warriors. Note the elongated ear-lobes so important to the Masai.

Mother and child. A baby David, in a beautiful dress, with his proud mother (circa 1922)

Going home for Christmas. David and his mother, returning from his first term at school at Ngaramtoni.

David (centre) and two of the Findlay children – barefoot in the Serengeti (1929)

Masai cattle clamber down hewn steps to a watering hole at Ngasumet.

Milking time in a Masai manyatta.

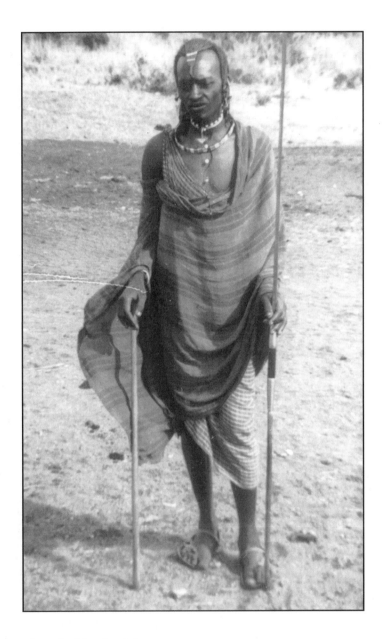

A typical junior Moran.

David collecting water at a stream running across the 'new' Arusha-Ngorongoro road (1933)

WILD DOGS & PORCUPINES

not take any of the immature bees, which I knew would not be acceptable in our house. I noticed Matanda and one of the other boys bending down and peeing on to their hands. This at first rather shocked me, but they said it was the usual form of washing after collecting honey as it got rid of the uncomfortable sticky feeling. Needless to say, I did the same and felt quite clean afterwards.

On reaching home that night I found that our one and only white farming neighbour, Mr Trichardt, who lived nine miles away over the mountain, had come by ox wagon to visit us and collect groceries and spares. He had brought his eldest son Lexi, and I was invited to return with them when they left for home at mid-morning the next day. I was happy to accept, but disappointed when they refused to take Matanda too: in their opinion 'kaffirs must stick to kaffirs, white boys to white boys'.

By about four in the afternoon we were still some distance from the Trichardt farm and the oxen were beginning to tire.

We had reached the second Waso crossing and Mr Trichardt ordered that the trek oxen be outspanned and watered. They were also given an hour to graze before we moved on. When darkness fell a Dietz lantern was tied to the centre of the leading yoke and a man sent to walk in front. This, I learnt later, was solely to give the leading oxen confidence and to avoid any stampede in the event of a lion or leopard appearing on the scene.

It was eleven before we arrived at the farm, after one of the most enjoyable rides I have ever had. There had been a lot of animals along the route, ranging from herds of impala, zebra, eland and wildebeest, to the odd lone hyena. Occasionally the trek oxen had stopped and turned to sniff the wind - an indication that something a little more dangerous was close. However, when this happened, someone would walk up and down along each side of the cattle and with a couple of swishes of the whip the team would be off once more.

While I was at the Trichardts an incident occurred which, although it now appears amusing, was not at all funny at the time. Several months before, on one of our trips to Arusha, we had run out of water and were unable to refill the radiator of the old Ford, which had leaked. So my stepfather ordered everyone to urinate into a can, which we used to top up the radiator. Matanda and I thought it a great joke but as soon as the engine heated up the stench became unbearable and froth poured out of the radiator. We eventually reached our next point of call mainly, I think, on the little water left in the radiator and not on the urine, which is not to be recommended as a cooling agent for any engine. It was with this incident in my mind that I went to bed one night at the Trichardts. I dreamt that I was once again peeing into a four-gallon can and woke suddenly to find the bed soaking wet. I was so ashamed that, before anybody had got up, as soon as it was light, I picked up my .22, called my three dogs and left.

On my way up to the forest I fortunately met one of the Trichardts' woodcutters who asked me where I was going. I told him 'Home'. When the Trichardts woke up and missed me, and heard what the woodcutter had to say - and found my wet bed - they put two and two together. They sent a man to follow me and, although two hours had elapsed since my departure, he reached our house ahead of me, creating great alarm.

After leaving the thick forest on the southern side of the mountain, I had decided to take a short cut along the ridge to the east and above where our farm lay. The track led through dense grass and small clumps of trees where buffalo and eland grazed. On reaching a point directly above our house, I followed a footpath down towards it. A mile from the house the dogs ran off barking. The grass here had been grazed down and was not all that tall, so from five hundred yards I was able to see quite clearly the dogs turn and come tearing back to me followed by a pack of probably two hundred wild dogs.

I had heard what wild dogs could do, and without hesitation I flung myself into a small copse and climbed one of the trees. I got myself into a good position from where I could see all around, and as the wild dogs got closer I shot four of them. No sooner had they been shot than their mates attacked them, in one instance before the wounded animal had even fallen. The smell of blood incensed them and they began fighting among themselves.

My dogs, in the meantime, came straight for the tree I was perched in. I had only five rounds of ammunition left and was not going to part with them unless it was absolutely necessary. Luckily the wild dogs decided not to wait for me to fall into their open mouths and instead chased my dogs down towards the farm. Within a hundred yards of it the brutes gave up and disappeared into the forest.

Some servants saw my three hounds return without me and this increased the tempo of the panic, but after a while, with yelps and barks the dogs made their way back up the hill in search of me, and orders were given to follow them. Having seen the wild dogs go off, I had climbed down and was cautiously moving from tree to tree towards home; I was very nearly there when I saw my dogs and the servants approaching and I immediately regained confidence.

On arriving at the house I had to explain why I had left the

Trichardts and made up a lot of stories to hide the real reason - uselessly, for Mrs Trichardt had already written to my parents telling them what had occurred. I was sent back the next day to finish my stay with Lexi. The bed-wetting was not mentioned, even by the children, and I have never known whether they had been told or not.

Shortly after this experience I had a good opportunity to see what could have happened to me had I been caught by the wild dogs. My stepfather (who, to restore my morale, had said he would now rather I called him Otto) and I were driving to Wasonyiro, and on the verge of a hill, some five miles out of Soitsambu, the turnboy knocked on the roof of the cab and pointed to a pack of wild dogs, at least a hundred strong, chasing a small herd of eleven oryx. We stopped and clambered up on to the hides loaded on the back of the lorry to watch. A dozen or so dogs had by this time split the oryx herd into two, nine going in one direction, which the dogs abandoned to go after the other two. These they also split, concentrating on just one. Now a fresh group of dogs took over and manoeuvred the lone oryx within an area of a square mile. Every three to five minutes new groups relieved those in the chase. When the oryx began to tire one of the dogs managed to get a bite in between its hind legs and abdomen. This immediately slowed it down and in a flash the whole pack was on it. It still stood, braying and terrified, while its intestines were ripped from its body. Then it fell, either dead already or from the sheer weight of the dogs.

We were unable to drive any closer as there was a small ravine between us, so we never knew exactly how long it took the dogs to devour the oryx completely, but we had had the satisfaction of seeing the poor creature kill two dogs before it collapsed. One of them was still impaled on a horn when the oryx fell.

When I returned from the Trichardts, having spent a further four days with them, it was midday, and Matanda had walked up the hill to meet me. He was in a highly excited state and said we must go at once to a porcupine hunt. This was too good an opportunity to miss, so I told the servants who had been sent to escort me home to tell my mother that I was back, but had gone away again to kill porcupines.

Matanda then told me what was afoot. Apparently porcupines had been raiding the gardens belonging to Government employees, who had followed them and discovered where they were lying up during daylight. The usual practise when a porcupine hole is found is to search for all the outlets. Sometimes these are as much as sixty yards from the main entrance and there are often two, three or even more. The holes are then covered with chopped wood, which is set alight, leaving one outlet around which everyone waits for the porcupines to emerge. This is a most effective system as the smoke and heat soon drive the animals out, whereafter they are speared.

If no one wants the meat - which is most unlikely, even though the Masai do not eat it - all the holes are blocked and fired and the porcupines die underground. On this occasion a professional porcupine hunter, a Msukuma from Lake Victoria, had volunteered to go down and bring them out alive. This seemed to me, and to most of the people there, a lot of nonsense and we just could not believe that anyone would venture down a porcupine hole.

Large crowds had congregated around the twelve entrances. As the hunter was keen to catch all the porcupines alive, traps only were set outside each hole and no fires lit. The traps consisted of gunny sacks, each with a small hole the size of a porcupine's head cut out at the end. The bags were then expanded with three wooden hoops inside and placed with the larger opening to the burrow entrance, thus forming a tunnel. The pressure of the animal forcing its head through the small hole at the end where it could see daylight would collapse the hoops, and the porcupine would be held fast as its quills would prevent any backward movement. This method works very well.

However, on this day none of the porcupines made a run for it, so the expert undressed and, armed with a stick an inch thick and two feet long, together with a six-foot length of rope, he went down the hole. The entrance to a porcupine hole is so narrow that only a small person can possibly squeeze through, and it amazed me that this man - by no means small - could wriggle down and disappear so fast.

One of his helpers had been told to listen for instructions, but we heard nothing, and after about five minutes the catcher emerged saying he would need a machete as there was an obstruction in the tunnel. There were, he went on to say, a lot of porcupines, but he did not know how many. He then informed the crowd that there was also a very large snake down the hole. This impressed the people immensely, although this sort of story about a snake, so I am told, is not always true. The professionals like to make out that they and the snakes have a special understanding whereby they do not interfere with one another, and the tale is believed to be a myth to discourage others from attempting to practise their craft.

The man, now carrying the machete and the rope, proceeded down the hole again. We could tell roughly where the porcupines were from the outside as we could hear him digging. Suddenly the digging stopped and from the surface we could hear him and the porcupines scuffling about. The roof of the tunnel could not have been more than a foot under the surface as we heard quite clearly the noise of the porcupines' tail rattles, which they always make when excited. The rattling stopped and shortly afterwards we saw two feet; followed by the man's body, emerging from the hole. He was pulling on the tautened rope and as he came out a porcupine appeared at the end of it.

On seeing the people it raised its quills ready for battle, but the man grabbed it by a front leg and said something to it whereupon its quills immediately flattened and he shoved it head first into a sack which he tied up. The amazing thing was that the porcupine seemed quite content with its lot, not even scuffling about in the bag.

This process was successfully repeated seven times, and when the hunt was over each porcupine was removed from its bag, tied upside down by the hind legs to the branch of a tree and knocked on the head. The killing completed, the expert and two of his fellow tribesmen had the carcasses carried away. Then the crowd was told to move away from the holes so that the catcher could prepare the burrows for their new occupants. These, he claimed, would arrive in a very short time. This we could well believe, as porcupines move about within a certain area and often return to holes that have been used in the past.

When the hunter and his helpers thought everyone was out of sight, they carried out a ceremony of spilling something at the entrance to each hole and with a branch brushed the earth clear of any tracks and footprints. They then picked up their sacks and went away.

Needless to say, Matanda and I had watched all this, hidden behind a bush, and when the men had gone we went over to see what they had done. Whatever it was that they had sprinkled around the holes must have been very light as we could see no trace of anything and all marks had been erased.

There are two points of interest worth noting here. One, that more porcupines did indeed return to this particular hideout, and the other that, during the entire episode I have recounted, not one single quill was dropped. This is rather surprising, as when you kill a porcupine, even if you shoot it cleanly through the head, there are invariably a number of quills scattered about afterwards.

Some time later Matanda and I met and made friends with a young fellow belonging to the same tribe as the professional porcupine catcher. He told us that he too had been down porcupine holes and brought the creatures out. He offered to show us how to do it, so off we went to a series of holes which we knew to be occupied. With us went two other boys, all of us keen to try our hand at the art.

The Msukuma boy went down first, but came up saying there were no porcupines there at the moment, although there had been within the last few days. He knew this because of the smell, which still lingered - a smell in the nature of an unclean lavatory. He then suggested that we each go down the hole in turn with him, just to get the feel of it. Matanda went first but only got as far as his ankles; he said the hole was too small for him - which was rubbish, as he was smaller than the Msukuma boy. He refused to try again, saying that holes were made for porcupines and snakes and certainly not for Masai. I got a little further than Matanda - at least my feet disappeared from view - but with a sudden mixture of claustrophobia and downright fright I decided to leave porcupine hunting to the experts and shot out of the hole.

The Msukuma youngster told us that the medicine used to bring out the porcupines was obtainable only through the catchers and he did not know what it was nor could he acquire it, except for use in the presence of the catchers.

Jock MacDonald had given my mother a recipe for porcupine meat, which was reputed to be delicious so, having been presented with one by the Msukuma, Otto was determined that we should try it. The preparation entailed removing all the quills and dropping the porcupine into hot water in the same way as for a pig, and then scraping off the outer layer of skin. The intestines were taken out and the meat then cooked like pork. The meat is very rich and has a strong pork-like, gamey taste. We smoked some, quite successfully, and I am told that if cured properly it makes extremely good bacon and ham.

CHAPTER FOURTEEN

MATANDA IS EATEN BY A LEOPARD

*L*ATE ONE NIGHT, WHEN WE WERE IN BED, a car drove up to our house, followed by a lorry. There was a knock on the door and a shouted 'Hodi, is there anyone in?'

Otto got up, calling 'Ngoja! Wait and give me a chance to get dressed.'

When he opened the front door a man with a thick foreign accent inquired if he was Mr Fischer, as he had been told in Nairobi that my stepfather would be willing to take him hunting. The stranger was invited in and it now appeared that he was not alone, for a figure stepped in after him, completely enveloped in scarves, coats and other wrappings, scarcely recognisable as a human being, let alone a woman. This was Madame.

My mother got up and lit the lamps, and the gentleman introduced themselves as Monsieur and Madame Michel Mauchaufee from Paris, come to hunt and photograph wild animals in Africa. Such exotic visitors were rare in our part of the world, but my parents took it all in their stride and food and camp-beds in the sitting room were quickly provided.

The following morning the Mauchaufees pitched camp about two hundred and fifty yards from our store, in a coppice just off the road, and there they stayed for some six weeks. This was their first visit to East Africa and neither could speak much English, but we all got on together very well, our family picking up a bit of French and the Mauchaufees a smattering of English mixed up with Swahili.

At this time we drew our water from a spring about a mile and a half away in the forest. This water was perfectly safe to drink, but the Mauchaufees would not hear of it, as they had been told that all water in Africa was dangerous. Their lorry, after off-loading and servicing, was sent straight back to Nairobi for stores - consisting mainly of soda water, which they used not only for drinking and cooking but for washing their faces too. Both of them were at this stage very particular about their skins and finger-nails, and consequently went about most of the time smeared in oils and creams to protect themselves from the sun and dirt. Monsieur Mauchaufee especially was meticulous about his nails and these were manicured regularly every day. This fascinated the Masai and me, and although Otto became the Mauchaufees' great friend, he just could not take their fastidiousness and was inclined to snap at them at times.

By the end of six weeks they had weathered down considerably and, although they would not drink anything other than soda water, they at least began to cook the occasional dish with local water.

A pride of lion lived close to the Loliondo trading centre and had become quite tame, although there were rumours now and then that they had killed a person or animal in the nearby Masai manyattas. These stories were not true but because of their proximity to human habitation the lion were rather a nuisance, as they would saunter about looking for food. Those to blame for this were Otto and various members of the Government staff who used to shoot meat for the lion and dump it near the stores. The lion came to expect this service and if they were hungry they would hang around roaring and frightening people.

One night while in this mood they visited the Mauchaufees' camp and caused quite a furore, as the French couple had not as yet had any experience of lion at close quarters. The incident occasioned an evacuation of the camp and the Mauchaufees moved into my room while I made do on a camp-bed in the sitting room.

My stepfather had now finished planting his maize and was able to take the Mauchaufees on safari. They had a successful fortnight's shooting from a camp they set up at Waso. They both got a lion each, a couple of buffalo and a rhinoceros. They also bagged numbers of small game animals. Monsieur Mauchaufee shot a leopard and although his wife had an opportunity to do so as well, when she saw the leopard in the lights on a kill, she just could not bring herself to shoot it.

The Mauchaufees were very full of themselves when they returned to Loliondo and had gained considerably in confidence, so much so that they no longer insisted on Otto remaining with them in camp at night. They had to return to France shortly after this, as they had children at home and wanted to be there for the holidays. Their equipment and lorry were left with us pending their return. This was not as soon as had been planned, but they did come back within the year. By the end of their second visit they had become quite accustomed to the hazards of Africa and had forgotten their fears concerning water. Soon after this they suffered a reversal to their fortunes and, when we were forced to go to the Lupa, they arrived there too, and joined in the mad rush for gold. They no longer had unlimited funds and in a short time they became very down-to-earth people. So far as I know they never returned to live in France.

Matanda came one morning to tell me his father was moving his manyatta to another place fifteen miles north-west of Loliondo on the Waso river, and that he would have to go too to help in the move, but would not be away for long. I thought it would be difficult for him to visit me from such a distance in future, as he would have nowhere to eat and sleep. He seemed quite surprised that I should consider this an obstacle and said, 'What about all the other manyattas? What's wrong with them?

'Well,' I said, 'they don't belong to your father.'

He laughed; saying it made not the slightest difference who the manyatta belonged to. Provided there was food and somewhere to sleep, which there always was, and provided he complied with the rules of etiquette for his age-group, he could stay in any manyatta he wanted.

I was allowed to accompany Matanda on the move, on condition that I returned the next day. On the morning of the move I awoke while it was still dark and without washing, and wearing shorts, shirt and pullover with rawhide sandals of the type worn by the Masai, I picked up my .22 and walked off to meet Matanda. By the time I reached the manyatta about two miles away, it was just beginning to get light and the women were still milking. As soon as they were finished the mature cattle moved off with the elders, morans and the bigger layonis, leaving the donkeys, the very old men and women, the small children, younger layonis and the women and one or two able-bodied elders. The donkeys were caught and loaded with every conceivable thing: water-bags, hides used for beds and for partitioning the huts, cooking utensils, and all the heavier possessions. Next, the women carrying their breakables, such as calabashes, and their babies, moved off alongside the donkeys. Matanda and I waited until they were safely on their way then, with an elder and two other youngsters, hurried ahead to join the advance party.

The cattle did not move fast as they grazed as they went, and shortly the women and donkeys passed us. We ambled on and as we came across manyattas, some of our party, mainly elders and morans, would call in for a drink of milk or water and then catch us up later. We reached the new manyatta just before dark. When I asked Matanda why the cattle moved so slowly he said that apart from letting them graze, there was no need for haste as the boma was already constructed, although as yet there were no houses: these would not be necessary as it was the dry season. In any case, the building of the houses was the women's work and would be done in their own time.

It is unusual for the Masai to have to construct a new manyatta as they normally move from one back to another, and it is just a question of patching up the fence surrounding the huts and the huts themselves. In this instance, however, Matanda's father had earlier suffered a bad outbreak of disease among the people, so the original manyatta, about two miles away, had been burnt down. This is customary when there has been an epidemic, whether among the humans or the stock. The new manyatta was sited on a well-drained quartz hillside, protected from the wind and situated about a mile from water. The hill was covered with a great many extremely large rocks and huge cave-like breaks in their formation. Some of these extended twenty to thirty feet into the hillside and in one of them lived a family of leopards.

The donkeys had been unloaded and small shelters of hide put up where the huts were to be built. This was all done by the women, helped by their children. The elders did condescend to bring a few bits of wood to light a fire near where the huts were to be; but, having done this, they sat down and ordered the women and youngsters about until the calves arrived, followed by the cattle. This diverted the elders' attention, as there was nowhere to pen the calves and they had either to be tied up or held by the children while the cows were being milked. This the women did immediately and when they had finished, they made sure all the calves were taken from the cows and put in a safe place surrounded by hides so that they could not suckle during the night.

What impressed me throughout was that, although the women did everything except herd the stock, there was at no time any sign of strain or extra exertion on their part - and no complaints. In fact, if someone had not known that the Masai did not move every day, they could easily have taken this as a normal daily occurrence.

The next morning I left to walk the fifteen miles back to Loliondo. Looking back, and knowing what I know today, I would not care to do this same trip, at that age, by myself, again. However, at that time I was so used to being alone in the bush that it did not even enter my head that I could meet with any danger, although the area was teeming with game of every sort.

Two days later, when I was swimming in the river, a Masai moran I knew came running up shouting, 'Debbe! Debbe! Come and see Matanda! He has been eaten by a leopard!'

'What do you mean?' I yelled back.

He repeated, 'He has been eaten by a leopard!'

I asked if Matanda was badly hurt and where he was; the moran said, 'Hurry! Hurry! He is with your mother. You must come and see he gets properly treated with medicine!'

When I was told he had been carried the whole way from the new manyatta, I realised he must have been badly mauled as it was unlikely that he would be carried unless he was completely incapable of walking. The Masai do not consider open wounds, unless they are extremely bad, to be of any major significance, nor do they have any respect for pain caused by wounds such as these. In the case of unknown sickness and witchcraft, their attitude is the reverse.

I ran all the way back to the house with only my shorts on, leaving everything else by the river. Matanda was lying on the kitchen floor, flat on his stomach while one of the servants helped my mother remove bits of loose skin and dried blood from his back. As a first-aid measure the Masai had smeared the wounds with cow dung, and this too had to be wiped off. The whole of his back was lacerated and looked as if someone had drawn a sharpened rake down it. He had a particularly nasty gash high on his left shoulder which my mother thought was probably a bite. During the entire time that his back was being cleaned Matanda did not moan; nor did he flinch at any stage although it must have been extremely painful, carried out as it was without any form of anaesthetic. He was running a very high temperature too. Any average human being would never have recovered, and my parents were quite convinced that he would not live.

After my mother's treatment, which took about an hour-and-a-half, he was laid on a bed and given aspirin with hot, very sweet tea. He slowly began to recover and tried to tell me what had happened, but at this point my mother put her foot down and I was told not to disturb him on any account.

The following day Matanda was much worse and groaned each time he tried to move, but his temperature had dropped and my mother thought his chances of recovery were better than they had been. On the third day he showed a big improvement and was able to talk.

The Masai have great faith in the white man's medicine when applied to open wounds or given by injection. In orally administered medicine they have some faith, but less, and will often turn to the witch-doctors for not easily diagnosed ailments. On this occasion Matanda was quite convinced that he had been saved even before the treatment was complete. And now he told me his story.

Matanda and two layonis had taken the sheep out to graze when suddenly the flock panicked and scattered. He saw a leopard take a sheep and drag it into a cave on the hillside near the manyatta. One of the layonis leapt at the leopard and speared it, causing it to drop the dead sheep just inside the mouth of the cave. As the boy now had no weapon, Matanda gave him his own spear and told him to look for another opening to the cave. Matanda then pulled out his simi and, armed with that and his heavy club, entered the cave. All he could see was an opening at the far end and he shouted to the layoni outside to keep an eye on it. All of a sudden the leopard leapt on him and in the dim light of the cave he had no chance to do anything other than plunge his simi through its shoulder, and turn to run for the exit. But the leopard was too fast for him and pounced on his back, knocking him down. It clawed him, making great sweeping gashes and biting deep into his left shoulder; then suddenly it collapsed. The other boy came running in and speared the leopard, narrowly missing Matanda, but the animal was already dead, with Matanda's simi through its heart.

Five days later Matanda was walking about, although a bit stiff; on the eighth day he and I were busily engaged in building a game-watching lookout in a tree, and this activity was followed by a fairly hectic hunt. So his recovery continued without any setbacks, however, the deep wound in his shoulder took the best part of two months to heal completely. The leopard had left its mark. The last time I saw Matanda, six years ago, the scars were still very much in evidence.

Matanda's extraordinary recovery, in the days before penicillin and antibiotics, points to another incident which occurred much later on and which gives a good indication of the mentality of the Masai and the psychological effect of injury and disease. Many years later my wife and I were driving away from a cattle market in central Tanganyika at a place called Chenene in Gogoland, when we were stopped by a large group of Masai standing by the roadside. On investigation it appeared that they had been in a battle, and one of them had been speared through a lung. This man had walked fifteen miles to the main road before dying.

Among the five others wounded was a moran who had been slashed across the head with a simi. The top of his skull was completely cut away from the brain cavity, and my wife, who is a nurse, discovered that there was just a small hinge of skin holding the top of his head on; when this was lifted, the brain could be seen pulsating. We were amazed that he had travelled all that distance on foot and was still alive, but my wife did not think he could live much longer. Another of the injured had a superficial spear wound in the chest and, more serious, the calf of one leg cut away. The third man had a broken forearm which had to be amputated later, while the fourth warrior had been badly knocked about and bruised but appeared not to have any grave injury. The last had a slight cut on the arm, but the long lobe of one of his ears had been sliced through.

We had room in the pick-up to take only the three most seriously hurt to Dodoma, while the other two followed an hour later on a lorry. My wife was at the time working at Dodoma hospital, so we were able to follow the progress of the Masai. Four of the men were eventually discharged - including the moran with the visible pulsating brain; but it was a different story for the Masai with the cut ear lobe.

When he was first admitted to the hospital, the staff was very busy, and as his ear had already started to fester, and as he was the least injured, the doctors, instead of repairing the lobe, cut it off, leaving the moran with a jagged edge to his ear. For the next four months the hospital had endless trouble with the man, then he died. As there was nothing physically wrong, the doctors put his death down to the psychological effect of losing his beautiful ear lobe. His dignity had been mortally offended and it would have been impossible for him ever to recover.

CHAPTER FIFTEEN
RAIN-MAKING

*W*HILE MY STEPFATHER WAS TINKERING with the engine of the Ford one day, one of our regular visitors, a Masai laibon of the rain-making clan, became far too inquisitive and kept getting in the way. He was told several times to move back but, being a Masai, he was insensitive to any instructions and within seconds his head was back under the bonnet. Otto got rather annoyed, especially as the engine was not behaving as it should. He turned to the laibon and said, 'You are supposed to be a rain-maker. Now push off and make rain, and stop bothering me. And if you can't make rain, I'll do it for you, but you'll have to give me the cattle you are usually paid for doing nothing.'

In true Masai fashion, the witch-doctor retorted, 'If you are so clever and think you can make rain, why don't you?'

'All right,' said Otto, 'sit down there for two minutes and I'll sort out your rain troubles.'

When he had finished his work on the car, Otto called to my mother to bring a mug of water with two small packets of Epsom salts dissolved in it. Otto gave this to the laibon to drink, having first obtained the Masai's promise that any cattle due to be paid to him for making rain would be handed over to Otto. The laibon then drank the Epsom salts and was told to go home. When all the filth and hypocrisy of his trade was cleared from his body, Otto told him, he could come back.

Otto thought that this was the last we should see of him, but next day he came with two layonis leading a nice fat lamb. It was obvious we were going to have rain in the next few days as the weather was very hot and sticky and the right cloud build-up had taken place. Also, rain had been reported in the vicinity; added to this was the fact that the rains were already overdue, so my stepfather could expect a modicum of success.

The fat lamb was offered to him as a token gift, and the laibon assured him that he had been purged so many times that there could not possibly be anything left which could interfere with my stepfather's witchcraft. He could therefore go ahead and bring the rain - if he knew how. To this taunt, Otto replied with a ten-minute lecture on rainmaking European-style, and to cover himself in case of failure, warned the witch-doctor that if he had not cleared himself out completely, the witchery would not work. At this point the laibon had to dash off to the nearest bush. 'The fiftieth time!' He yelled as he vanished.

When he returned Otto asked him if he had done anything and he said, 'No! Because there is nothing left but the pain!'

Otto then told him to climb up and sit on the mudguard of the car, but to take off his toga-like cloth first as it might be caught in the fan. This he did, with Otto holding one of the spark plugs in his right hand and the Masai's shoulder with his left. As soon as the shock went through the laibon he shrieked and broke contact. Otto made him come back, and the process was repeated about five times until eventually the Masai was jumping around like a jack-in-the-box, screaming his head off and laughing at the same time. Otto did not turn a hair and took the shocks through his own body without any reaction. At last the man was told to go home and to drink only fresh milk for two days, by which time, if he had done all he had been told, it would rain. But if it did not rain it would mean that not all the bad spirits had left his body and he would have to return and go through the same treatment again. My mother was sorry for him and gave him something to stop his diarrhoea. That night we had a cloudburst over Loliondo and the rain continued for a fortnight without a stop.

Now that the rains had started we knew the game would move in, so Matanda and I, with a gang of Masai boys, decided to take the dogs and go hunting. On the way we met an Oldorobo who said he knew where to find two cheetah cubs whose mother had been speared, and he described the place to us. He said the cubs were very small and could not have wandered far from under the acacia tree where their mother lay dead. The place was about a mile away, and we stopped to cut some wild bark rope to tie up the three dogs, otherwise they would have rushed in and killed the cubs long before we could catch them.

When we got to within sight of the acacia tree Matanda and I waited, holding the dogs, while the others went on to find the cubs. The dogs picked up the scent and were very difficult to control as they were not used to being tied up. One of them broke away and went straight for the tree which the other boys had just reached. A cheetah cub which had been suckling its dead mother was rescued just in time from the jaws of the dog; but it proved to be a little fiend and scratched at the face and arms of the boy who held it. The dog went berserk, jumping up and trying to snatch the cub away, so I had to leave Matanda with the other dogs and dash to his aid. This was disastrous as no sooner had I gone than the dogs broke away from Matanda and joined in the mad skirmish of shouting boys and spitting cub. I called to the boys to hit the dogs and they managed to keep them off until I got there. Meanwhile the cub had been wrapped up in a loin-cloth which kept its claws out of the way. The dogs then set upon the dead mother.

We looked around for the other cub and found it in the fork of the tree, about seven feet up. We tried to get the dogs away in case it fell down, but without success. The Masai boys did not fancy catching the second cub - they had had enough of being scratched - and suggested pushing it out of the tree for the dogs to have. 'After all,' they said, 'we have got one cub and do not need another.' I had to promise to steal one of my parents' sheep to take to an olpul if they would keep the dogs at bay while I went up the tree. I took off my shirt and climbed the tree, but as I tried to wrap the cub up, it fell. Luckily Matanda had his loin-cloth ready and grabbed the cub before the dogs could get it. This little creature had an injured leg and was very frightened, but after struggling for a short time it became quiet and meek, as did the other.

We carried our new acquisitions home in a sling made from a loin-cloth tied to a pole, but on the way we ran into a storm and had to shelter under some trees. We were there for about two hours, wet and miserable, and trying to keep the cubs warm. Just as it was getting dark the rain eased off so we pushed on home. I transferred the cubs to my shirt; by this time it looked as though they would both die, particularly the one with the hurt leg. Matanda and I made a run for it and reached home before the rain started again. I was about to have my ears pinned back in a big way for having gone off, as usual, without permission, but when my mother saw the cubs and heard the story of how we had saved them, all was forgiven and I was complimented.

The little cheetahs were put in a box next to the fireplace, and after about an hour they began to recover and show signs of life. For the first two days they would not touch food of any sort. My mother had contrived a bottle for them with a teat made from leather, and once they started to suck there was no stopping them. The problem was how much to allow them, and how much water to add to the milk. We relied on my mother over this, and she must have been expert because in no time at all they were doing well and had begun to eat meat.

About a fortnight later, Jock MacDonald came to see us and he advised catching birds to give to the cubs whole as there was something in the feathers that was necessary to the cheetah diet. He said we should not give them plain raw meat without the skin and intestines otherwise they would become lame in their hindquarters. This we did and the cheetahs eventually grew into two fine specimens, and the best pets we ever had.

When fully grown, they accompanied Matanda and me, with the dogs, on some of our hunts. They were idle hunters themselves as they were too well fed at home, but often when our sheep were out grazing, with buck nearby sharing the grass on an open plain, the cheetahs would use the sheep as cover to stalk the buck. Then they would make that terrific short charge for which cheetah are famous, and bring down their prey.

They were virtually house-trained within a month of being rescued, and moved about the house as if they owned it, getting into every chair and bed. In the early morning, when my parents' tea was carried in to them, two bowls of milk were also taken into the bedroom; and, after lapping it up, the cheetahs would jump on to the double bed and there play and purr like a couple of overgrown kittens. When we left Loliondo they were handed over to the Veterinary Officer, who released them on the plains.

The witch-doctor, who now strictly speaking owed Otto somewhere between five and ten head of cattle, was not seen in the area for a long time. He had, together with a number of Masai tribesmen who had heard of the incident, decided that my stepfather was a very good rain-maker. When he reappeared some years later during a famine and asked Otto to make rain, my stepfather said he could not do it again as the laibon had not paid his debt and was therefore unreliable. The laibon offered to pay both what he owed and for the next lot of rain in advance, but Otto decided to hang on to his reputation and would not dabble in rain-making again. Nor would he accept the offer of payment for his first effort. For a long while afterwards the Masai could not understand why, when he could make rain so easily, he would not do it again. To this day some of the old men who were at Loliondo at the time still maintain that he brought rain, and he is often referred to as the 'Lashomba (white man] who brought rain'.

CHAPTER SIXTEEN

MASAI WEAPONS

ETWEEN OUR FARM AND THE RANGE of hills to the north was fairly heavy forest country, mainly olive and cedar. On the tops of the hills were large rocky outcrops where thousands of hyrax lived. These little creatures are about the size of a rabbit, and have small rounded ears and large eyes. In a number of characteristics they resemble a lot of larger animals, and are said to be allied to the elephant in particular. I and my friends used to spend hours competing with one another as to who could kill the most. The Masai used a tiny proportion of the skins - as only junior laibons wore them, sewn together as capes - so I took the majority which we had made into blankets, or karosses, which we gave to friends or kept for ourselves.

We discovered after a while that unless you hit the hyrax with an arrow in the brain or stunned it with a knob-ended arrow, there was absolutely no chance of recovering either the arrow or the hyrax because as soon as the little animal was hit it would disappear down a crack in the rocks. We therefore devised a new system which entailed getting very much closer to where the hyrax sunned themselves. This was either after a shower of rain in the afternoon, or in the very early hours of the morning, a particularly good time being a sunny morning after all-night rain. We would choose a spot no more than six or seven yards from where the hyrax sat and, armed with an arrow and a piece of string about ten yards long tied to the barb of the arrow-head, we would wait. If we were successful and hit one, a quick jerk on the string would pull it off balance and then we would rush forward and hold it before it could get off the barb and vanish. My best catch for a day was four, and Matanda was not all that successful either, but a little Oldorobo boy who sometimes went with us bagged eleven in one day.

After being out one day for more than three hours without any luck, Matanda got up and announced that he was going home - he was fed up with hanging around for hours without catching anything. So we followed him, and by chance came upon a honey-bird which led us, after an hour and a half, well over to the east and behind the forest. Normally in the wet season we avoided the forest because of the rhinoceros, but this day we went through it as it was the quickest way home, and also Matanda had been instructed by his father to collect wood for making knobkerries.

The Masai knobkerrie is made from an olive sapling and the joint where it grows from a branch or the trunk of a tree at roughly a right angle. When cut from a reasonably sized branch, the work entailed is not considerable, but the final result will not be as good as when it is made from a sapling joined to the trunk. The reason for this is that a kerrie cut from a branch consists of a large amount of white wood which is both lighter and more inclined to rot than the wood of the trunk which is matured. So a kerrie cut from the trunk, if the handle is, say, one and a half inches thick, will have most of the white wood shaved off and the whole of the knob will be solid, hard wood. This is very popular but does mean a lot of work, both in the cutting out and in the shaping which often takes as long as a month to do.

For a long time I had wanted a black truncheon, so while we were in the forest I cut a suitable piece of olive, and over the next few days Matanda helped me season it by cooking it in the earth under a fire. This can only be done a little at a time, otherwise the wood dries out too fast and cracks. I then skinned it and left it for about six weeks, having rubbed it all over with beef suet. The next stage was to shape it partially by chipping at it with a hatchet. It was once again covered with suet and left untouched for at least another month, at the end of which I made the finishing touches to the shape with a pocketknife. This I followed by scraping the surface with a piece of metal or broken glass, and when the club was completely rounded and properly shaped I put a piece of sandstone, crushed as finely as possible, into a skin and sanded down the club.

The treatment for a knobkerrie is much the same. When finished, these weapons can either be left as they are or coloured black to give an ebony effect. This is done by pushing the kerrie or club into wet black cotton soil and leaving it there for a week. When pulled out the wood is blackened, and this black colouring penetrates to nearly a quarter of an inch if left in the soil long enough. It is difficult for a layman to distinguish wood treated in this way from true ebony.

Witch-doctors and chiefs carry a small knobkerrie for show which is carved out of a straight piece of white olive and is always very carefully done. At first appearance it would seem to be machine-made. This knobkerrie is blackened and is carried only as a status symbol.

Matanda also told me how the two different types of Masai sword, or simi, are made. The first, probably the most common and most useful, uses the good-quality imported machete as a basis. It is filed down to a rounded point at the tip and sharpened on both sides. A lot of work goes into making one of these, and probably the use of three or four files. The wooden handle is then rounded and from the tip of an ox-tail a piece of skin is cut while still wet. This is forced on over the handle and bound with thin string. When dry, the ends are tidied and the string removed. This gives a ridged effect, and also, of course, a better grip to the handle.

The other type, which is the true simi, is made by the traditional spear-makers and is similar to the spear except that it is narrower at the handle and broadens at the end. This weapon, like the spear, is usually of very inferior quality metal, but it is highly valued and carries great prestige amongst the Masai (as against the better quality product imported from Britain and normally sold to tourists who believe it to be the genuine article).

The scabbard for both these swords is elaborately made, but not very efficient and requires re-making every now and again. A soft wood is cut and two boards thinned down to nearly a sixteenth of an inch. This is done with a pocketknife. The boards are dried and made to measure for a particular simi. They are then tied together with strings laid in patterns over the boards, together with any old buttons and beads the maker fancies. A calf-skin is prepared by placing it in mud until the hair can be scraped off without difficulty. It is then laid over the pieces of wood, with the simi inside, and sewn up. The pattern made by the strings, beads and buttons will show through the skin when it has dried and stretched. The bottom end is tied and the top edges are turned over and into the scabbard.

The finished article is painted with a bright red dye and left to dry for two or three days. The loop for the belt is also made when the calf-skin is wet. The end result is a very smart-looking scabbard, rather Roman in appearance. However, care must be taken when removing and replacing the sword, and the scabbard should never be gripped around by the hand, as the weapon will very often cut right through the calf-skin.

CHAPTER SEVENTEEN

GOLD FEVER

*W*E HAD FOR SOME TIME BEEN financially insolvent, although this situation was kept from me. Over the years of the depression our shop at Loliondo and the one we had opened at Soitsambu, twenty-two miles away, had shown heavy losses. This was disappointing for my brother Norman who had been put in charge of the Soitsambu shop on his return from school in England. Our crops, too, although on the whole fairly good, had not been realising economical prices because of the slump in the prices of grain in Kenya. In consequence, ground maize-meal flour, ready for sale from Kenya, could be put on the market at Loliondo at a lower price than we could grow it. The future therefore did not look at all encouraging to my parents, and something had to be done.

At about this time there were stories of farming families packing up around Arusha and Moshi and going south to the gold strike on the Lupa, and these rumours prompted my stepfather to make a trip to Arusha purely to investigate the facts. He was away five days and on his return told us we would be moving off to the Lupa within the month. Arrangements were made for Daniel to remain and look after what was left on the farm and we, with a couple of our servants, would go to seek our fortunes on the diggings. If and when we had accumulated sufficient capital to put the farm on a proper footing, we would return to Loliondo.

Although this new venture appealed strongly to me, I was most anxious about Matanda and we approached my parents to ask if he could go with us; but there was no question of it, and Matanda's father would no doubt have stepped in and refused to let him go in this particular instance as the Lupa was far down in the south-west of Tanganyika.

The journey took five days and the newer of our two lorries was loaded with every possible thing it could carry. My parents sat in front and Norman, the two servants and I perched on the back with Mother Hubbard, our grey Persian cat, in a little box. She caused some anxiety when, having produced a litter of kittens on the journey, she was found to be missing. Otto and Norman had heated words about who was to blame and we had to go back ten miles to retrieve her. We also broke our rear axle, but by some miracle an identical half-shaft was found in the District workshops at Mbulu, and the District Officer, with the only other two European men there, used the occasion to have a party on the roadside, bringing their wives and drink with them.

When we arrived at Kungutas, we met Bill Martiniglio whom we knew from the Wasonyiro days. Bill, called Bwana Chai by the Africans, as he drank tea continuously, kept a shop which supplied the diggers with their day-to-day requirements. He also owned two lorries, which at this stage he ran between Mbeya, Chunya and Kungutas. He had a very young, attractive Afrikaner wife, and we stayed with them for two days while we equipped ourselves before proceeding to the Lupa River, where we camped.

With five Nyachusa labourers we started prospecting along the river-bed, but by the end of the first month we had virtually exhausted our capital, with very little gold to justify the expenditure. My stepfather, however, took the matter lightly and pointed out that any experience gained was not for nothing.

We now increased our labour force to thirty and Otto worked out a system whereby a man had to produce a certain amount in order to qualify for a month's wages. If he managed to do so in a day, or a week, he could then sit in camp until the end of the month if he wished, and would still draw his full month's wages. If, on the other hand, he wanted to continue working, he would be paid on a laid-down bonus basis for the balance. This system allowed my stepfather a very small margin of profit per worker, and we therefore had to take on more men in order to make it worthwhile; but the workers liked the scheme and within a very short while we had a labour force exceeding two thousand and were doing quite well.

In the meantime my mother had decided to go back into the business she knew best, and with the help of Bill she opened a small hotel in Kungutas, named Tudor House, after the one she had run in Mombasa. It proved reasonably successful and we were now overcoming our financial troubles.

The Lupa in those days, although much less primitive than Loliondo, was certainly not, by any standards, modern or comfortable. The climate was poor and diseases of all types prevalent. Living conditions were primitive as everyone lived in tents or, more usually, grass houses. During our whole stay there we lived either under canvas or rough thatch, with mud floors. There was no fresh food to be had - everything either came out of cans or was dried. Fresh meat was hard to come by as the country was heavily infested with tsetse fly. Game was also scarce on account of the number of people and the climatic conditions.

The road between Mbeya and Chunya, over the Mbeya range, had only just been completed. Prior to this all supplies to the gold fields had been carried by porters, great trains of them, numbering up to two hundred men, arriving daily from Mbeya. The only licenced liquor store was at Tukuyu; a caravan of porters might start out with half a dozen cases of whisky and end up at its destination with less than one case, and a sheaf of IOU chits.

The digging fraternity was a very friendly and co-operative one on the whole, and consisted mainly of people who had failed financially elsewhere for various reasons. They ranged from commoners to titled remittance men. Many were down-and-outs, but some were wealthy individuals out to increase their fortunes, or purely there for the sake of adventure. There were married men with families, but most were bachelors or had left their wives behind; there were even some single females come to seek husbands and fortunes. With very few exceptions they were all tough and prepared for any eventuality. One day they would be rich, having struck gold; the next day they would be penniless. Usually, when a digger struck gold, one of the first things he would do was to pay off his debts to friends, merchants and pubs. If he were lucky, he might have something left over, in which case he went to the Goldfields Hotel where he drank away most of his money with his less fortunate friends. Government officials sent to this area were carefully selected for their ability to deal with the prevailing situation.

It was the custom of the day for those who were hard up to be helped by the more fortunate. So much so, that, later on, when pubs started appearing in places like Chunya and Mkongilosi, a man in the money may have paid for ten or even fifteen of his mates' drinks and accommodation for a week or more. Drinks were sold not by the tot but by the bottle, and if there was anything left over it was measured and credited to the customer. Often a digger would walk in, put down a bag of gold containing anything up to ten ounces, and say to the hotelier, 'When that is finished remind me to go home.' Anyone coming into the bar for a drink would be served and, even though he may never have met the depositor, his drink would be paid for out of this deposit.

A small school for about fifteen European children was opened at Chunya, with Miss Boshoff, one of my old teachers from Ngaramtoni near Arusha, in charge. Arrangements were made for children to stay with people in the vicinity of the school, and as we were some distance from Chunya, I lodged with Miss Boshoff. The building was simple, with the teacher's study and a storeroom at one end, and desks, slates, pencils and exercise books being provided by the parents. I remained at this school for a term and a half; when I left I had a total of one year's schooling.

Shortly after the advent of the road to Chunya it became quite a town. A bank was opened, a butcher's shop, bottle store, hotel, hairdressing salon, a ladies' dress shop, a Government hospital and a private nursing home, and concrete buildings with corrugated-iron roofs began to pop up all over the place.

The methods for extracting alluvial gold were becoming more modern and more numerous. A few very rich strikes were discovered, and the areas where this happened became hives of activity for a while, with most of the diggers spending their time chasing both genuine and imaginary strikes. One of the exceptions was my stepfather, who continued working to a set method, using large sluice boxes and working the river-bed in the dry weather and the banks and higher ground during the rainy season. He never struck any very rich outcrops of much size, and the largest nugget I can recollect him finding was seven ounces in weight, which he got from the dry blower; but he continued steadily to make a good living and became quite prosperous.

Often, having pegged a claim on one day, Otto would be approached by someone the next day and told to get off. At first he thought he had probably made a mistake, but he soon learnt that some so-called prospectors did no prospecting of their own – they merely followed the more successful diggers and over-pegged their claims. This they did either by pulling out the pegs and destroying them, or by moving them. There were only two really effective methods of dealing with such people. One was to give them a good beating without witnesses; the other, if the claim was considered a valuable one, was to refer the matter back to the beacon inspector, who would sort out the trouble. As soon as a claim was applied for, an accurate sketch-map, giving the exact location of the beacons, had to be submitted to the Mines Department. Provided this was done correctly, the over-peggers soon packed up.

During this period there were many outbreaks of malaria which developed into fatal blackwater fever. One of the victims was a bachelor from Saza, who happened to own a new Chevrolet boxbody car into which his friends put his body. They drove him to the Goldfields Hotel at Chunya and left him parked outside in the car while they went in for a drink. At intervals each one in turn went out to see how he was getting on, taking the odd bottle of whisky to give to the corpse. This went on until the following day when someone decided it was time that the death was reported and arrangements made for the funeral. The miner was buried that evening with all his untouched bottles, and a number of new ones, placed beside him. Three days later his friends ran out of credit and started to dig up the grave so as to have a drink with their pal. Unfortunately for them, the local District Commissioner heard of this and they were removed from the cemetery and sent home.

The activities on the Lupa had gained momentum and were flourishing, and new people of all kinds flocked in from different parts of the world. Some lasted only a few months, and others stayed on, sometimes for several years, and little towns began to spring up. Large mining organisations moved in and underground reefs were opened up. With this new influx of adventurous people came also the less honest types and illicit gold buying began to show its ugly head.

During our first few months on the Lupa, a rather amusing incident occurred, although it was very upsetting for my mother. Otto had come home for the weekend from the diggings as usual, and had brought two small aspirin bottles filled with fine gold. As my mother was going to Chunya the following Monday, these were left in her care to deliver to the bank, which was the official gold buyer for the area. She was lectured about not losing the bottles, so instead of putting them in a safe place, she carried them around with her in her cardigan pocket. On Monday morning before going to Chunya, she visited the long-drop and somehow let one of the bottles fall down the hole. She was naturally in tears, and after discussion with some friends it was decided to break the lavatory down and empty the pit.

It was a hotel lavatory and, as can be appreciated, was used by a lot of people, so the amount of excreta and disintegrating newspaper that had to be removed before the bottle could be found was quite considerable. It had to be spread thinly over the ground and a rake used. The operation from beginning to end took five days, after which a new long-drop had to be built. The smell persisted for about three weeks, and my mother's hotel lost a lot of business, more than the value of the gold.

Just before Christmas my mother was besieged in the new loo. She had bought three turkeys for fattening, and these were shut up at night but allowed to roam the hotel grounds during the day picking up scraps. One of them was rather fierce and liked to chase people, biding his time and catching them unawares. The long-drop as yet had no door, only a screen, and the turkey cock followed my mother in and attacked her while she was sitting down. She shouted for me, and picked up the wooden seat to try to fend the turkey off with it. After grabbing the turkey I could do nothing but laugh at my mother, her trousers and knickers round her ankles, peeping through the hole of the seat and screaming her head off.

A lot of funny things happened on the Lupa, which were told and retold in the bars, but tragedies also occurred. Kungutas was a few miles from a road junction known as Piccadilly Circus, and just down the Itigi road lived a young miner and his wife. They had not been in Africa long before they acquired a leopard cub which they reared successfully and kept for two years. It was very tame and spent its days playing with their dogs. The couple eventually had a child, and one morning, when the father was at work, the mother went out on to the verandah to pick up the baby, who was then about five months old. To her horror she found the leopard cleaning itself, having eaten the child.

At no time had the leopard shown any signs of being vicious, and had on many occasions played with bigger children. It had many opportunities of killing puppies or chickens, but had chosen to be quiet and well-behaved at all times. It was of course immediately destroyed and the grief-stricken parents left the country.

Generally speaking, the diggers were tough, carefree, cheerful and generous. Other than drinking, fornicating and prospecting, there was very little to occupy their time, particularly in the evenings, and the natural outcome of this were large gambling groups in each area. At the end of a three-day session at Makongolosi, when a wealthy miner had lost everything except his car and his wife, his opponent (who was keen on the wife, who he knew) suggested that he might put his car in the game on the basis of double or quits. The losing man refused, but said he would put his wife in. The challenge was accepted, the wife was lost to the winner and the game ended happily, one supposes, for all concerned.

After a year and a half on the Lupa, my stepfather had saved a bit of money and decided it was time to move back to his great love, farming at Loliondo. With the capital he had accumulated, he felt that success was inevitable, and added to this my mother had received a good offer for the hotel. My parents were not really cut out for the Lupa life and I suffered from continual bouts of malaria, a fact which in

later years paid dividends, as I seemed to build up a resistance to it. Norman, who had never got on with Otto, was now serving an apprenticeship in engineering at the Saza mine and was doing quite well and preferred to remain where he was.

After our equipment and hotel were sold we had fifteen hundred pounds capital and a new boxbody car, and this was considered sufficient finance to start up our farming venture on a sound footing. As a parting gift Norman gave me his .256 Mannlicher rifle as he had no use for it at Saza. I thought this was most generous and could hardly wait to get home to Loliondo to try it out.

Although the Lupa had done us well, there were no real regrets on leaving, except that Norman and I were parting for what appeared to be an indefinite period. We left before dawn and travelled at a good pace, arriving at Itigi at four o'clock where we filled up with petrol and water in the village. The station-master tried to persuade us to stay in the rest-camp but for reasons best known to my parents they preferred to slum it amongst the mosquitoes three miles further on, and that night Africa and her bug population were at their worst.

The next day trouble started forty miles on, with the car boiling over and no water left. We eventually reached some waterholes five miles short of Singida, where we camped, as we were all tired and tempers were getting frayed. Minor repairs were done on the car in the morning and we drove into Singida where we stayed for two days while the car was being fixed.

We had no more trouble on the journey and arrived in Loliondo three days later. John Pride, our old friend the District Officer, had gone on leave, but Drag Cartnell the Veterinary Officer was still there, although about to be replaced by a Scot. The Indian shopkeepers were the same, and Daniel (who had left the farm) was back offering any help he could give us. He was now, amongst other things, working for the Administration at the local dispensary, having been on a short course for dispensation of ordinary, day-to-day medicines, and was recognised by all as the local doctor. Most of the work which we had started on the farm a year and a half before had deteriorated to the extent that we had to begin again from scratch. Our house was in such a state that it could not be lived in. All the windows were smashed, most of the corrugated iron had been torn off the walls, and the only materials we could salvage were the timbers and corrugated iron from the roof. Our implements and machinery had either been stolen and sold, or had disintegrated beyond repair.

Work was begun immediately on a new house and farm buildings, and new machinery brought in from Nairobi. Cattle for use as trek oxen were bought and our former Lumbwa and Nandi ox drivers appeared from nowhere to start training them. In a very short while farming began in earnest. In that first year after our return from the Lupa, we planted a hundred and seventy acres of maize and harvested a good crop, which was a giant achievement considering the limited facilities and machinery available to us.

One of the first things I did was to send a message to Matanda, but he did not appear. I made continual enquiries about him, but was told he was busy, that he would come when he could get away. Meanwhile I met up with some of my other Masai friends and began to get about a bit.

Our original dogs had been given away to friends when we left Loliondo, so now Otto got me three pups similar in shape and size. We also had two dogs we brought back with us from the Lupa. These were a bull-terrier pup and a wire-haired terrier called Whisky, which was Otto's dog and went everywhere with him. The other three and the bull-terrier accompanied me, although they were all still very young and not much assistance when hunting; but now of course I had Norman's .256 Mannlicher, which was sufficiently new to me to be more interesting than my old .22.

Hunting one day a short distance from home, I shot an impala, and while I and my two Masai friends were feeding the dogs with the liver (to make them brave and used to hot blood) three Masai youngsters turned up, one of them Matanda. At first he did not speak, but after a few minutes he asked me how far away the impala had been when I shot it with my new gun. When I told him anything up to two hundred yards, he would not believe me and wanted me to prove it. So we arranged to meet the next day to test the efficiency of the gun. He seemed quite friendly and gave me news of his family and where his manyatta was situated. He said his sister, only a little older than Matanda himself, had died two months before in childbirth. When I said, 'But she wasn't married,' he replied, 'No, but she was married and circumcised before she died so there was no disgrace to her or the family.'

It was not until some time later that I discovered why Matanda had not come to meet me when he knew I was back, and his manyatta was only a short distance from my home. He had apparently expected me to do something about taking him to the Lupa, and for a long time thought I would come back to fetch him. When this did not happen he was convinced I had deserted him, and his attitude hardened when other Africans told him this was the way of Europeans who, when they got tired of playing with blacks, discarded them. Matanda felt very bitter and could not forgive me until he had actually seen me and learned the truth. This turned out to be the beginning of a second and far more binding and mature friendship between us.

CHAPTER EIGHTEEN

THE WITCH DOCTORS

ONE DAY WE VISITED AN OLPUL where we knew all the participants, and were immediately offered meat. While eating I heard a discussion regarding our local laibon who had been asked to bring rain. There was to be a meeting of elders in a few days' time at which the witch-doctor would be presented with five head of cattle. He would then decide whether or not he was ready to bring rain. The father of one of our moran friends had been ordered to provide an ox, and he complained that this was the second time in succession that he had had to do so. He naturally felt it was someone else's turn, but the others at the olpul thought it was just because he had far more cattle than anybody else in the area and would therefore benefit the most when the rains came.

Matanda and I were out hunting the next day and had not had much success. We were just about to give up and go home when Matanda pointed to an impala about seventy yards away. I lifted my .256, aimed and shot the buck in the neck, killing it outright. Just then an elder moran who had heard the shot approached us and Matanda showed him the bullet, saying, 'There must be some witchcraft in these ndiols for a small piece of metal could not kill an animal in an instant like this.'

I had meanwhile been thinking about the business of the witch-doctor bringing rain, and turned to them: 'Nonsense! We Europeans don't go in for witchcraft, and anyhow there's no truth in it!'

'Do you not believe it?' replied the moran. 'There's a lot to it, and you will see when the witch-doctor comes that he will bring rain on the day he says.'

'What if he says there will be no rain?

'That he might do, if the cattle given to him are not suitable, or if he is not pleased with them; in which case we will have to hold another meeting at a later date.'

'I don't believe in it,' I said. 'And in any case, where does a witch-doctor come from and who makes him a witch-doctor?'

'Well, I'll tell you,' said the moran, and settled himself down comfortably to tell us the tale.

Years ago two morans went up into the forest for an olpul. One was from the Ermamasita clan's new subclan known as the Molelyan, and the other was an Ilbargeneti clansman. After slaughtering their animal one of them went to look for herbs deep in the forest, and there he found two very small boys. One of these children was of a light colour and taller than the other, who was very dark and had a protruding coccyx. The second boy was immediately named Ngido'ngoi, which means 'tail'. As the children appeared to have no parents, the two morans decided they would each take one back to their families. Ngido'ngoi was adopted by the Ilbargeneti moran and the taller, paler boy, now named Kileken, was adopted by the Molelyan moran.

As the boys were of an age to carry light loads and were sensible enough to understand instructions, the morans used them for various tasks. After a few days it became apparent that Kileken was an exceedingly clever boy - so much so that the morans began to be disturbed by his intelligence. For example, when the boys were sent for water or wood, Kileken would return in a very short while with a large load, whereas the other child took a long time and brought only small amounts, more in line with his age. One morning they were both sent off for herbs and before the morans had time to roast a rib, Kileken was back with every type of herb, some of which had not been found in this forest before. Ngido'ngoi returned after about three hours with nothing, saying he could not find any herbs.

On the following day the morans went home with their two adopted sons and told their people of Kileken's extraordinary abilities. The elders said they were exaggerating, that a small child the size and age of Kileken could not possibly do what was claimed of him. The little boys had never before drunk milk, but Kileken took to it immediately, whereas Ngido'ngoi became ill and was unable to drink milk for quite a few days. This in itself made the people think there might be something in what the morans had said.

One morning the two boys were sent off to look after the calves in their respective herds. After two days it was reported that Kileken was quite capable of looking after the herd alone. This he did, and did it very well from then on; so well that the calves grew at twice the rate of any others and none died. One day when one of the morans was sick, Kileken volunteered to take out the mature cattle to graze. That evening the cows gave twice as much milk as they had ever done, and more cows were reported to be in calf. Also, three calves had been born without mishap. This was amazing in a boy of his age. From that time on he herded the cattle and they were always in better condition than any other herd; they produced more calves, and the herd was never raided by animals or enemies.

After Kileken had been doing this work for a season, he told his adopted father that, provided he was left alone with the cattle and that at no time would his father approach without giving warning, the herd would always do well. If his father wished to come and look at the animals while they were out grazing, he must call to warn Kileken that he was coming. (To this day the Masai have a special call when they are approaching a manyatta at night - this was the call that Kileken gave to his father).

By the time Kileken had reached the age when he was to be considered for circumcision, his father had become a very wealthy man. When other cattle were dying through drought, Kileken's herd thrived; and when other cattle could not sleep because of the heavy rains, Kileken's herd was always on dry land.

After getting very drunk one day, Kileken's father decided to go and look at the cattle he had been boasting about, but he forgot to warn Kileken and approached him from the rear. As he spoke to his son he saw that the herd was feeding on lush green grass - and this was during a bad drought when other herds were dying of starvation.

'My father,' said Kileken, 'why do you do this when I have warned you not to come without calling first?'

At that very moment there was a rumbling, roaring sound like thunder and Kileken turned into a flame which shot up into the air and disappeared in the sky. The cows began to abort and the grass withered; and Kileken was never seen nor heard of again. In a few months his father was left with a herd of less than a hundred head; but it was said that any man who drank milk from those cows that remained was able to converse with the bird called Oldilo, and this bird had the ability to foretell the future.

Ngido'ngoi became a quiet, respected young man, marrying at a late age, as his adopted father was not a wealthy man. One day at a celebration he got very drunk and while in this state of intoxication stood up and told the elders he had seen a vision that the year to follow would be one of drought and famine such as the Masai tribe in all its history had never experienced, and that they would lose so many head of cattle that they would have to go to war to compensate for their losses, or else the tribe would die of starvation. He told them that from that day on they were to accept him as the greatest of laibons. But the people would not believe him and ignored his prophecy, although he warned them further that, when the drought began, they were to come to him before they grew too weak from hunger. He would instruct them in detail as to what they were to do to overcome the disaster. 'I do not want any of you to believe in my special powers until you have seen with your own eyes that they exist and are true.'

The following year was as he had foretold, and when the drought was at its worst all the elders of Kisongo met and agreed to use the powers of Ngido'pgoi. They went to him and told him the whole of the Kisongo tribe would put their faith in him and do what he instructed.

He immediately ordered a meeting of the morans to be held outside his manyatta on the north-eastern high point of the Ngorongoro Crater. When they had assembled he told them to pick out three of the fastest-walking morans, those who could walk long distances without tiring, who were to go in an easterly direction until they found a moran called Lobilogonya. This moran, of outstanding physique, was to be their leader, but Ngido'ngoi could tell them no more about him as he had never met him, nor did he know exactly where he lived - only that such a man existed. Ngido'ngoi said the remaining warriors were to round up others from all the clans of the Masai, and they were to meet together, with cattle for slaughter, in the basin of the Ngorongoro Crater on the first night of the full moon. There too the elders of the clans were to bring their young maidens of mature sexual age for the morans' pleasure before they went to battle.

On the night stipulated, his instructions were fully carried out and there were so many morans that they almost filled the crater. Eight of the most prominent elders were chosen and ordered to fetch the hide from the sacred slaughtered ox. This they did.

Then they chose the most beautiful of all girls, of perfect physique, bred from a disease-free line, and whose parents were properly married according to custom. She was led into the middle of the arena and asked whether she had ever had sexual intercourse with anyone other than a moran, to which she replied 'No!'

She was then asked if she had ever had sexual intercourse with anyone of her own clan. Again she answered . 'No!'

Ngido'ngoi then said, 'You are fit and worthy, and you have not lied. Choose the moran you most fancy from amongst the thousands here and present to him the string of beads you wear around your waist.'

The girl inspected the warriors and on reaching one particular moran, she looked him over very carefully, took off her beads, tied them round his waist and said to Ngido'ngoi, 'I choose this one.'

The young man was summoned before Ngido'ngoi who asked him his name. According to Masai custom his friend replied for him: 'His name is Lobilogonya and he comes from Loitokitok on the slopes of the White Mountain (Kilimanjaro).'

Ngido'ngoi then said to him, 'you have been chosen as the worthy leader of all the Masai morans. You shall now lead them into battle to recover all the losses this drought has caused. Provided you do as I say and follow my instructions carefully, you will come back alive with most of your warriors, and henceforth you will be the leader of all morans of your age-group.'

He then told the eight elders to hold up the hide from the sacred ox and make an arch, with four elders on each side. 'Lobilogonya! See the arch there of worthy elders and a worthy hide? You are to lead your morans through it and you are all to travel in a southerly direction for four days and three nights, and on the evening of the fourth night you will see smoke. Until you see this smoke, just before the sun goes down below the earth, not one of you is to look back towards Ngorongoro; and if you have obeyed me you will see an oldilo (the talking bird) in a tree. You are to stalk it very quietly and as soon as you catch it, you are to shout "Saiboku!" and the bird will at once turn into a human. You are then to ask Saiboku where the local tribes graze their cattle and he will tell you. You must comply with all his instructions and promise him protection. That is all I have to say to you. The elders will decide when the battle is over what my services have been worth, and from then on all successful battles will be paid for, to my appointed successors, in the same way. Now go!'

The morans began to file through the archway, led by Lobilogonya, and they were still going through when the sun was in the middle of the sky.

When they reached the oldilo bird in the tree, all happened as had been foretold. Saiboku showed the morans the Mbulu tribe's cattle grazing in a valley and advised them not to attack until night fell as the Mbulu were frightened of the dark. The battle raged through the night, and the following day, when the Mbulu had been chased away, the morans took all the cattle and the young girls and boys, and returned to Ngorongoro. Lobilogonya gave back his string of beads, and the girl who had presented them to him became his wife.

Ngido'ngoi, who already had one son, predicted that he would have another with only one eye, and it was to him, Ngido'ngoi said, that he would hand on his powers, while his first son would have none at all. A third son was also born and his name was Sembeyo, and he too possessed the powers of witchcraft.

The son with one eye was called Batian and, after he had succeeded his father, was laibon for two full moran age-groups. One of these groups, the second, was known as the Ndorossi, because they frayed the lower edges of their loin-cloths. They took it unto themselves to prepare for battle in an area now known as the Londorossi on the slopes of Kilimanjaro. At this stage in their history, the Masai under Batian were prosperous and the morans had no difficulty feeding themselves on nice fat bullocks, but after a while they became impatient and restless for battle. Rumours of impending raids by other tribes kept reaching them but never materialised. Not to be caught unawares they devised a signalling system whereby hides were cut into thin strips and joined together to form a long rope to which cow bells were strung. This hide rope extended up the mountain slope over a distance of six miles, and the procedure was for the alerted warriors to pull the rope, thus warning their immediate neighbours who would in turn warn the next group, and so on.

But the bells never rang and the impatience of the morans could no longer be contained, so they donned their battledress of vulture-feather shoulder cloaks, black ostrich plumes on the tips of their spears, bells round their right legs, shields painted with the different clan signs, and head-dresses-some of lion-skin, some of black and white ostrich feathers and others of grey.

Batian was at a place called Nduimet bordering on the moran encampment, and one morning the senior moran pulled the rope and ordered all the morans to congregate in the Nduimet glade.

Messengers were sent to ask Batian to attend the meeting, and when he appeared he was told that the warriors were bored and unhappy at not going to war and would remain quiet like women and layonis no longer.

At this point a strong tall moran, who was not a leader of any sort, stood up and cried 'Batian! Batian! We want to go to war!'

'You think you can fight?' asked Batian.

'Only cowards think! It is not you who are going to be killed, nor is it you who will never again pierce the red flesh between your wife's thighs at night, but us. We demand that you prepare us for war!'

This annoyed Batian exceedingly, but he knew he must not make a false move or he would be killed, so he gave his consent, but warned that success in battle would elude them as the time for going to war was not ripe. He then went home and instructed his wives to take out all the hides and carrying-frames used on the donkeys and to spread them on the ground, killing all the cockroaches individually as they appeared. 'As you kill them you must shout out "That's another one of Batians' warriors killed!"'

He further instructed them that only one cockroach must be spared, and this one he appointed his chief wife to protect.

Having given these orders to his women, he went back to the morans and told them to go to war against the Lumbwa tribe in Kenya. So they went to battle and the whole age-group was annihilated, except for one man called Nalamanbot, which means "the one who can defeat three manyattas on his own", but when he returned home his name was changed to Kilamariot, which means "the servant of women".

He did not like this at all and refused to take orders under his new name, so Batian cast a spell over him and he entered the shell of the remaining, protected cockroach, and therefore survived the next Lumbwa raid.

The Lumbwa, having defeated the Masai, decided to follow up their success by killing off the few remaining morans, who for various reasons had not gone to battle, and most of the elders. They took back to Lumbwa the remnants of the Masai herds, leaving only twenty head which they did not see. Their anger against the Masai was intense and they returned once more the next year to kill all the young males they could find and remove to Lumbwa the females of breeding age, leaving behind only the old men and women.

After the Lumbwa raiders had gone, the survivors, fearful that they might return yet again, agreed to approach them and beg them to leave the Masai alone as they were no longer a foe for the Lumbwa to worry over. They took with them all the calabashes as a sign that they no longer had women to clean them; the circumcising knives for both boys and girls as a sign that they no longer had youngsters to circumcise; and the blood-drawing arrows to show they had no cattle from which to draw blood. They also took the calf-, hyrax- and monkey-skin rugs - all of which indicated status - as a sign that they no longer had any status. Amongst all these things was Batian's cockroach. During the journey it dropped out and the spell was broken, and the cockroach became a young layoni.

CHAPTER NINETEEN

LENANA'S SPELL

OUR MORAN FRIEND HAD TALKED so long it was then almost dark and we had still to carry the impala home, but he promised to finish his story the next time we met. Matanda and I then removed the liver, kidneys and hind legs of the impala, leaving the rest as the complete carcass would have been a heavy load to carry all the way home.

I barely slept that night thinking about the story, and when I related it to my parents the following day they too were fascinated, and suggested I should go to hear the rest of the tale as soon as possible. So at midday Matanda and I took the dogs and went directly to the olpul. We found the moran lying in his bivouac talking to his ndito, and he was only too pleased to continue with the story. As it turned out he was an expert on Masai legends and was very happy to show off his knowledge in front of the other morans and their girls. He leaned back, folded his arms behind his head and went on with the tale of the vanquished Masai.

On arriving in Lumbwa country the elders produced the goods they had brought and explained the reasons for each item, begging to be left alone to die a natural death. The Lumbwa said they would agree on one condition. Having guessed that the Masai had a few cattle remaining, the Lumbwa set them the impossible task of bringing milk from Masailand with the froth still on it.

On the seventh day of their return journey the Masai elders met the layoni who had been Batian's cockroach. 'My fathers,' he addressed them, 'what was the outcome of your meeting with the Lumbwa?'

'What is it to do with you, layoni?'

'As we are in the same situation, surely it is better for me to know what is happening so that I can act accordingly. Otherwise I might be caught unawares, and also I will not know what is expected of me.'

So the elders told him about the milk.

'That should be quite easy,' the boy said. 'All you have to do is put milk into a calabash and when you get near the Lumbwa chiefs shake it well until it froths up.'

This they did, and although it was accepted by the Lumbwa they insisted on having yet more proof of their subservience in the form of a very large calabash full of fleas, brought to them within a set time. On their way home the elders discussed this, but none had any idea how it could be achieved. One of them suggested seeking out the layoni who had helped them before to ask his advice, which they did.

'Simple!' he said. 'Cut the black manes of your donkeys, chop the hair into tiny pieces the size of fleas, then wait in the Lumbwa country until you get a good windy day. Deliver the fleas, and when you pour them out of the calabash make sure you are upwind of the Lumbwa. The wind will blow the chopped hair towards them so they will move away and will therefore not notice that you have tricked them, but you will have fulfilled their requirements.'

The boy's instructions were carried out and everything went according to plan, but the Lumbwa required yet one more sign of the Masai's faith. They were told to go home and bring back a toothbrush made from the iron of the lower part of a spear.

The elders went home feeling very depressed, firstly because they thought they could not accomplish this task, and secondly because they felt it would not be the last demand made of them by the Lumbwa. They decided to consult the layoni again. He told them it could be done but would require time, and he said they should go back and ask for a year's grace. It was granted, and when the elders informed the layoni, he announced that he would have to be circumcised immediately, remaining at home only eight days after the ceremony before going into the forest. He requested that the elders go through what herds remained and find enough goats for him to feed on for a year.

After living in the forest for two months he called the elders together and told them to find all the knobkerrie makers still alive and to see that a start was made on making as many knobkerries as possible. By this time the new moran had built up his strength and soon he visited the knobkerrie makers in turn and tested their workmanship and choice of wood. At the first three camps he broke the knobkerries and gave instructions for them to stop work, but at the fourth camp he found the right club, unbreakable and of the correct weight.

A month before the day on which the toothbrush was to be produced, a delegation of elders was sent to inform the Lumbwa that they would be arriving to deliver the toothbrush on the date stipulated, and that all members of the tribe who were able to walk the distance would be accompanying them to pay their respects.

On the day the Masai elders arrived first and begged the Lumbwa warriors to receive the man, with his followers, who had made the brush, as they themselves had not been able to make it. The request was granted as the Lumbwa felt secure in their position of conquerors.

The new moran, during his stay in the forest, had collected together all the surviving layonis and had seen to it that they were circumcised. They were now his followers and they had been taught to speak Masai in a different dialect so that no one would recognise them as Masai. He had ascertained from the elders beforehand that the leader of the Lumbwa would be sitting on a raised seat, higher than the others, and that he had red eyes like the gum from a certain tree. The morans hid their weapons in their loin-cloths and their leader carried only his knobkerrie, the one he had specially selected. When asked why, he replied, 'A spear can slip and miss the vital part. A sword can strike a bone and be deflected. But a knobkerrie can only break from the strength being used behind it.'

When the toothbrush maker appeared before the Lumbwa, the Masai elders explained how they had persuaded this young man to make the brush. He meanwhile circled the Lumbwa leader, pretending not to be interested or to understand what was being said. Suddenly he saw his opportunity and raised his knobkerrie and struck the Lumbwa leader on the temple with all his strength, breaking the knobkerrie as he did so. A shout went up from the Lumbwa people that the toothbrush maker had killed their leader, and the Masai morans pulled out their weapons, and the Lumbwa took to their heels and fled.

On his return home, the young moran was sent for by Batian, who told him that he had done well, and that he would now be the leader of the warriors, and that he was to call them together and prepare for battle against the Lumbwa tribe. This battle he could not lose as he, Batian, would give his blessing. Shortly after this the Masai, led by the moran, conquered the Lumbwa and brought back all their surviving women, children and stock.

Batian had three sons by his first wife who were to follow him in witchcraft. The eldest was Nelion, the second Sendeu and the third Lenana. Sendeu decided to move from where the family had their manyatta in the Ngorongoro Crater as his elder brother Nelion would succeed his father as chief laibon; he went north into Kenya and settled at a place called Loita where he would have no competition from Nelion.

He told the people of Loita that he intended to make the area his home, and this was greeted with delight by the Loita Masai, as they had heard of the fame of this family of witch-doctors, and they immediately gave him more cattle and the free run of their country.

Although he did not say so, it was very apparent that Sendeu coveted the large herds his brother was to inherit, and in particular he desired a red and black bullock which his father had given Nelion because of his seniority. After Sendeu had established himself as a great witch-doctor in Loita, he ordered all the morans of this area, which covered most of Kenya and a small part of Tanganyika, to go to an olpul. When they had eaten enough meat and felt sufficiently strong and brave for battle, they were to send back a delegation of four leading morans to him. In due course this was done; when asked by Sendeu when they would be ready for war, they replied that the new moon was four days past, but when the next new moon appeared they would be ready to move.

Sendeu said, 'Go then, and collect as many waterskins as you can from the Oldorobo and fill them with beer for my elders and me to drink while I work at my witchcraft. All of you return here prepared for battle on the night of the new moon.'

On the appointed night the morans arrived dressed in their war attire, and a tall, powerful moran, bearing a sword-cut on the left side of his face, and able to lift three spears in one hand holding only the last five inches of the shafts, was chosen to lead the warriors. He was called Ol Lolkerindi, and Sendeu told him to go to Nelion's manyatta and bring back all his cattle and, most important of all, the red and black bullock. In the meantime Sendeu would cast a spell on his brother to keep him under the influence of drink until the raid was over - an unnecessary spell, as Nelion was a drunkard. But the spell could not have worked on Nelion in any case, as he was no longer the chief laibon. After their father Batian retired, Nelion, a hot-headed, quick-tempered man, chose to abdicate in favour of his youngest brother of whom he was very fond. Lenana was, by comparison, a quiet, very sound and popular man. It was therefore Lenana who was affected by the spell and he joined Nelion in his drunkenness.

It so happened that one of Lenana's morans, on his way to consult him, encountered Sendeu's warriors on their way to the north, already in possession of Nelion's herd with the red and black bullock. On his arrival he found Lenana and Nelion both drunk and boasting of their powers and their wealth. The moran told Lenana what he had seen and commented, 'What good are you when you allow all of your brother's cattle to be stolen?'

Lenana realised immediately that he was under a spell, so he removed it, simultaneously putting a spell on Ol Lolkerindi, who was at that very moment trying to force a lively heifer back into the herd. The heifer suddenly turned on him, killing him instantly. The leader of the raiding party was now dead and, as according to Masai belief no raid can ever be successful once the leader has died, the warriors relinquished the stolen herd and went home.

Only Lenana knew of the turn of events at this time, so he called a meeting of all the elders in the vicinity. They asked him to explain why he was not doing his duty as chief witch-doctor properly, and his brother Nelion said to him, 'If you are frightened of the responsibility and the power I have vested in you, you must say so now and I shall take them over.'

Lenana replied that he was not frightened, nor was he in any way incapable of carrying out his duties, and this he would prove. 'When my brother Sendeu left Ngorongoro, did I not stay to help you protect our tribe? I have been under a spell, but I ask your forgiveness just this once. If you do not forgive me, I have still the powers to give my brother Sendeu the power of light from both the sun and the moon and you would all be plunged into darkness.'

So Nelion and the elders forgave him, and Lenana fell into a trance. When he awoke he told them that if Sendeu assembled his warriors and tried to make war again, Lenana would know at once as his black cow with the white rump would calve, even though she may not appear to be pregnant. 'At which time I shall close all the leaks in his house and the only outlet shall lead to a spear.' (i.e. 'I shall surround him and his tribe with my warriors and have him killed.').

Just then his mother, who had come in with a calabash of drink, turned to Lenana: 'How can you allow an ordinary moran to kill your own brother, a man of his status? You are a man of power. Surely all you need do is to wipe out his warriors in battle and take away his wealth and leave him poor. He will then understand that he has done wrong and will come to you for forgiveness. This will make you much greater than having your brother killed by a lesser being.'

Lenana knew his mother was right, but a witch-doctor cannot retract a statement once made, so he picked up a stone from the fire in his mother's house and flung it at the wall, making a hole right through. 'You rat!' he cried. 'Get through that hole!'

The following year when his cow calved, Lenana called his morans to battle and gave them instructions first of all to surround Sendeu's manyatta with four rows of morans standing shoulder to shoulder. This they did, and when Sendeu and his family were panic-stricken, with no way through the wall of morans, a gap appeared which let him and his wives and children through, for Lenana had remembered his mother's words. The rest of the people in the manyatta were killed.

The battle raged on until the whole of the area under Sendeu's jurisdiction was defeated, and only then were Lenana's warriors satisfied. They returned to Ngorongoro with their loot and Sendeu was left a poor man, but he later went to his younger brother Lenana to beg forgiveness. Lenana not only forgave him, but allowed him to go back to Loita, giving him cattle and permission to practise witchcraft again. 'But', Lenana went on, 'you must never again attempt battle against me or my followers, and when I wish to go to war, you and the Loita Masai must throw in your lot with me.'

'Now do you believe in the Masai laibons?' Matanda asked me.

'I'm not quite sure,' I replied. 'Anyhow, it's a good story. But was that Sendeu any relation to the Sendeu who is now living to the north of Loliondo?

'It is he, the same Sendeu, although he is now an old, old man.'

Many tales were heard in our district regarding Sendeu's skill as a witch-doctor, and now that he was so very old, people wondered who could replace him when he died, for none of the younger laibons possessed his abilities and magical powers.

One evening the District Officer and my stepfather were discussing Sendeu's claimed success, and decided to try and make him prove his skills. They arranged to visit him the next time they went to Ol Bosimoru which was not far from where he was then living.

Arriving at Sendeu's manyatta, they were escorted to his hut and shown the usual Masai hospitality. They conversed on general topics, and then the Europeans began gradually to draw the old man out on his prowess as a witch-doctor. Sendeu was a great braggart and very proud of his successes, so he was only too pleased to discuss them. When my stepfather suggested that perhaps imagination or just luck played a big part in witchcraft practises, Sendeu offered to prove to them that this was not the case - but pointed out that they would have to make a reasonable request of him, something he knew something about and which was associated with the area and the Masai as a people. So Otto said, 'It is extremely rare to find an elephant in this area. Can you bring us an elephant, here?'

Sendeu replied immediately that he could, and told them that if they returned home by the same route by which they had come, past a pond, they would see three elephants in the pond. These they were not to disturb, and certainly not to attempt to shoot. If they came back the next morning, they would find only one elephant and, no matter how long they searched, they would see no tracks leading out of the pond. Also, if they remained at the pond, watching, the third elephant would eventually disappear, and they would not see it go; but he would prefer them not to wait for that.

The District Officer and Otto did as they were told, and in fact did see the three elephants in the pond. When they went back the next day, there was one elephant only, and although they looked all round the pond, they could not find a single track. They then left, not staying to watch the lone elephant vanish.

When they discussed this incident later with various Masai from the area, each man they spoke to told them that it was quite impossible for them to have seen any elephants as there were none in the area, nor had any elephant been known to come there in the past.

Both Otto and the District Officer, and the two African scouts who were with them, swore that their story was absolutely true, in every respect.

CHAPTER TWENTY

BESIEGED BY LION

*I*HAD BY NOW BECOME QUITE AN PROFICIENT DRIVER, although too young to have a licence. This, however, did not seem to matter much, as long as I kept away from towns. We had just gone through another financially difficult period. Our maize crops were extremely good but unfortunately, owing to the continuing slump, we were unable to sell the stuff at anything like a reasonable price. Eventually the whole crop - five hundred acres of maize - was sold to the Sonjo tribe through the Government, at fifty cents-a-bag in the field (sixpence in 1935), harvesting, bagging and other costs being their responsibility. Partly because of this and partly because of lingering malaria which he had been unable to get out of his system since leaving the Lupa, my stepfather was not well and my mother was not prepared to leave him alone in the state he was in. I was therefore instructed to take Sungura, who had now become a driver, and his turnboy to Arusha over two hundred miles away to collect stores.

The run into Arusha normally took two days each way, as the road was only a track as far as the Ngorongoro Crater. The first forty miles or so were over high, rolling country, sparsely wooded with acacia trees, with a water hole on the edge of the plains at Malambo. Up to this point the road had a fairly hard surface and was thought reasonable. It was not usual to go into Malambo as it was about six miles off the track, but it was useful during the dry season as a last watering point before tackling the next stretch - particularly with the avid water consumption of the old Ford. So on this occasion we called in there and filled up the radiator and our cans.

From Malambo the track led across the Serengeti Plains for a further forty miles, the first part of which was absolutely treeless and over very loose sand. During the dry season great care had to be taken to find the most solid ground as once a vehicle became embedded in the sand it could well be there for a whole week.

I drove over this section but just before leaving the sand at the far end of the plains, adjacent to the now famous Olduvai Gorge, I heard a thump from the back axle and the lorry stopped. On inspection we found that the rear half-shaft had broken in two, and it was quite obvious that nothing could be done other than to replace the shaft.

I discussed the situation with Sungura and the turnboy. It was clear that there would be no object in just waiting for help to turn up, as we could sit there for anything up to two weeks before seeing another vehicle. The only thing in our favour was that we had about fourteen gallons of water left and some food, but the full load of hides was a big responsibility. The nearest habitation was at Ngorongoro, about twenty miles away by road, though the turnboy reckoned it could be somewhat closer by foot.

The next problem was to decide who should go for help and who should stay, if anybody. Both Sungura and his assistant made it very clear that neither would stay with the lorry alone nor go for help alone. That left me with two alternatives: I could stay behind on my own or accompany them, leaving the lorry unattended. If I went with them and some Masai found the truck they would most probably cut off the tyres to make sandals. Also hyena could do considerable damage to the load of hides, tearing them down and having a good meal. So I decided to stay.

Then came the problem of the guns. We had a twelve-bore shotgun with two rounds left, and my .256 rifle with about twenty rounds. Because of the shortage of ammunition for the shot-gun I thought it best to keep the rifle and give Sungura the other gun. But when he saw that he would have only two rounds he refused to accept it, pointing out that I had at least the protection of the vehicle, whereas he and the turnboy would have to walk through lion country with no other protection. So the rifle it had to be.

The decision made, the two men prepared to leave as soon as possible as it was already midday. We quickly pulled the tarpaulin off the top of the lorry and tied one side to the roof, pegging the other side to the ground. We said our farewells, Sungura promising me that one of them would go on to Arusha, being away perhaps for three nights, and the other would return the next day if possible, with someone from Ngorongoro.

This part of the Serengeti is usually very windy, but on that particular day it was hot and muggy. At about four o'clock there was a cloudburst over in the direction of Ngorongoro, but I felt no more than a spattering of rain, just enough to lay the dust. Before it got dark I lit a fire and made some tea, and then arranged a bed for myself on the front seat of the lorry. The cab was wooden with half-doors, and canvas curtains for protection against rain could be rolled down but they were very dilapidated and gave little shelter from either rain or wind.

The place where we had broken down was, at certain times of the year, probably the most heavily lion-infested area in the whole of the Serengeti, which in turn has possibly more lion than any other game reserve in the world, and long before dark I saw a number of lion in the distance. This did not alarm me, as I was used to seeing and being very close to the Serengeti lion, which have a reputation for being quiet and not very interested in man. However, when night fell

I began to recall all the stories I had heard about lion, some of which were fairly gruesome; and to remind me further, every now and again I could hear them roaring all around. As the sound came closer I became more and more frightened. It is unusual for lion to approach a vehicle very closely at night, but for some reason, perhaps the smell of the hides or just curiosity, these came right up to within a few yards, so close I could see them moving about in the dark. To make things worse, they kept answering calls from as near as twenty yards away and these great roars at such close quarters were terrifying.

I thought of everything I possibly could to make them go away, including switching on the lights of the lorry, but the battery was rather flat and did not last long. At this stage I was sitting in the cab with the shot-gun in my hands, trying to see in three directions at once. The wind started up, whistling through the odd, lone tree. All of a sudden I heard a vicious tearing of the tarpaulin, and peering out I could see the lion which had thrust its paw through the canvas, not realising that it would not hold its weight. This scared the animal and there was a bit of a scuffle before it pulled itself free. I could contain my fright no longer and burst into tears, which I suppose helped me but certainly did not impress the lion.

The little scuffle must have scared them off temporarily, but only for five or ten minutes, then back they came. Some sort of game began, with these huge beasts tearing holes in the tarpaulin and tugging at the hides. My last semblance of control broke down when a lioness put her two front legs on the mudguard and pushed her nose to within a foot of the torn canvas curtain of the cab on the driver's side. I fired a shot right through the canvas, about twelve inches above her head, and there was a tremendous flurry before quiet reigned in the immediate vicinity of the lorry. I was now left with one round of ammunition and, completely dry of tears, decided that my end had come. It could not have been later than about half past nine.

The lion, for some reason, must have thought their little bit of torture had been sufficient as they did not come back until the early hours of the morning. I sat up the whole night wrapped in a blanket and clutching the gun, too shocked for more tears. It was bitterly cold, and the Serengeti wind grew in intensity, gently rocking the lorry. The canvas tarpaulin flapped and the ropes strained at the knots, creaking and snapping; and it seemed that the night would never end.

Just before dawn the roaring started up again. I was looking forward to the dawn, and had been doing so for what seemed like a lifetime. But the new spate of roaring initiated a fresh bout of terror, worse than the fear I had felt during the night. However, with the lightening of the sky I regained some of my lost confidence, and while sitting there in the cab, my courage returning, I saw for the first time a lion kill carried out according to the book, which, strangely enough, is rare.

A herd of about eight zebra was moving across in front of the lorry some fifty yards away, when suddenly three young lion charged them. The zebra panicked and swung back. They were in full gallop when a lioness who had been in hiding jumped on to the back of one, her forepaws and head on her prey's shoulders and neck. She then leapt off and lay down a little way away. The zebra collapsed and never made another move; it was stone-dead and I can only imagine that the lioness had broken its neck.

The lioness then got up and was joined by the three young lion, which began to tear the zebra apart. She merely sniffed the dead animal, walked off and lay down again. While the youngsters were feeding, two big brown-maned lions in beautiful condition came up to the kill, and the young ones respectfully moved away to lie beside what I now decided must be their mother. After a short while they got up and went a bit further away, the large males continuing their meal. An hour or so later, they moved still further, into the shade of an acacia tree, and there they remained until the evening.

The two males were approached at the kill by a scraggly, mangy hyena, which lay down at a distance, waiting for them to finish, and vultures also appeared. When the lion had had their fill, they dragged the remains - about a quarter of the zebra - twenty or thirty yards away. The vultures were getting braver and braver, closing in on the meat and being chased every now and then by one of the lion, which hung around until nearly eleven o'clock when they became bored and decided the game was over. They disappeared behind a sand dune and I did not see them again. The hyena took over the kill and, helped by the vultures, left nothing by midday except a few bones.

The kill I had just witnessed was entirely unlike others I have seen, and what most struck me was the speed at which it was carried out and the fact that the lioness did not feed on the meat at all.

I had by this time come to the conclusion that the friends of the night before, the ones that had caused me so much trouble, were the three young lion, and I now believe that they had no evil intentions, but simply found the tarpaulin rather fascinating to tear and pull about.

During all this time I had not once stepped out of the cab, but when the lion had moved off, nature forced me to brave it. I got out with gun in hand and inspected the damage. Apart from the tarpaulin which was torn to shreds, nothing appeared to have been touched. Having relieved myself, I felt a bit better, so I lit a fire and made tea. Meanwhile I wondered how I could possibly go through another night alone, if no one turned up to keep me company. Naturally I cast my eyes continually in the direction of Ngorongoro to see whether anyone was coming, and by about two in the afternoon I was very impatient and depressed as I was certain no one would come.

So I took the hatchet from the back of the lorry and chopped branches off the few nearby trees. These I piled up round the cab in preparation for the night, and while doing this I suddenly noticed dust about five miles away in the direction of the road from the crater. At first I was very excited, then decided it could not possibly be anything, as it was so unlikely that a car would be travelling along this road. However, as the little cloud of dust drew nearer, I began to think it might be a vehicle after all and my hopes rose. But then the dust vanished on a straight stretch where there were no hills. This was just too much, and I again burst into tears and went to sit miserably in the cab.

While in this state, through the sound of my blabbing, I heard an engine. I jumped out and there, less than half a mile away, was the Loliondo Veterinary Officer's Chrysler boxbody approaching fast. I promptly felt ashamed, thinking that Jock Gowan would laugh at me for piling branches round the cab, so I started to pull them away. When the car eventually reached me, I saw that Mr Gowan had with him the turnboy, whom he had picked up a couple of miles away. Apparently he had been on his way back, alone on foot. The point where I had seen the cloud of dust suddenly disappear had been at the moment they had met and Mr Gowan stopped the car. After I had related my tale to him, Mr Gowan turned on the African in some annoyance and said I should never have been left alone, but I explained that that was what we had arranged and that I was perfectly all right. I was feeling much better now in fact, and the terror of the night was fast receding.

We had an excellent meal that evening and I slept in the boxbody with Jock. The lion came back in force, but kept their distance. Jock stayed until the new half-shaft arrived two days later with Mr Singh on his way back to Loliondo. We found plenty to occupy our time during the wait, making little excursions from the camp we had set up. One thing we did was to go and check on the progress of the three moving sand dunes. I had heard people talking about them, and was naturally interested to see what was meant by their moving. These dunes are three large sand banks which, because of the wind, are continuously moving westward and, for reasons which I did not know, the Administration at Loliondo recorded the annual distance covered. This was so slight in my opinion that I quickly lost interest, but I have since then often wondered how far these dunes have moved, and whether they are still in motion.

CHAPTER TWENTY ONE

SHIELD MAKING

*W*HEN I ARRIVED BACK FROM ARUSHA with the stores, my mother told me that the District Officer had asked Otto to send his lorry to collect the mail from Narok. The postman had been taken ill at Ol Bosimoru, so he would have to be picked up on the way and carried to the hospital at Narok. Otto was still not well, so Sungura and I were sent, Matanda accompanying us for the ride. Matanda was very jealous of the fact that I could drive and he could not, and pestered me continually to teach him, which I would have done with pleasure, but Sungura was responsible for the lorry and would not hear of it.

The postman was an Oldorobo tribesman; his job was to go from Loliondo to Narok on foot - a distance of a hundred and ten miles by road, though slightly shorter by a footpath over the hills. He would leave Loliondo early on a Monday morning with his mailbag, which weighed anything from just a few pounds to sixty pounds. He would arrive at Narok on Wednesday evenings, collect the southbound mail on Thursday morning and be back at Loliondo by Saturday evening. This man covered at least two hundred miles a week with one day of rest, and he had been doing the job for over three years without a break, until this occasion when I took him to hospital (a week later he was discharged and returned to Loliondo with the mail). He continued with this job for at least two or three years more before it was taken over by an Indian contractor with a lorry.

On our homeward trip we had a little bit of trouble with punctures and a broken spring, and had to break our journey at Ol

Bosimoru. We stayed the night in one of the Indian shops, where the owner's wife fed us a wonderful curry. Also present were three well-to-do Somalis who had been round the district buying sheep and were now on their way back to Narok with well over a thousand animals. Somali traders usually came to barter for cattle, sheep and goats about three times a year, bringing with them blankets, beads, red ochre, sugar and hard cash, all of which was carried in donkey packs, some of the donkey caravans running to two hundred strong.

In the morning, just as we were about to leave, all hell was let loose as raiders attacked the Somali flocks. Guns were fired and the donkeys stampeded. One of the Somalis came running for help; at the best of times Somalis are inclined to panic and do a lot of shouting, and on this occasion they excelled themselves. When things had quietened down we, learnt that the raiders had got away with over forty sheep; two of the raiders, however, had been wounded and the Somalis were following them up.

One of the Somalis we had met the night before was seriously hurt with an arrow in his chest, and his friends brought him to us asking if we would take him to hospital. This put me in a predicament as I was already rather panicky about the whole matter and did not know whether I should go back to Narok - to the only hospital in the area, and eighty miles away which would take the whole day to reach - or take the man to the dispensary at Loliondo, which would get me into trouble for bringing someone from Kenya into Tanganyika, and where there were no facilities for dealing with such cases.

Eventually the head Somali solved the problem with the help of my host of the previous night. He said the man was obviously going to die as the arrow was in his lung, but anyway he would accompany him and me to Loliondo and hope to get help for the injured man there. Both he and the shopkeeper believed that the raiders were from Tanganyika, as they had fled in that direction.

A bed of empty gunny sacks was made in the back of the lorry and the Somali laid on it. His friend travelled beside him for the first five miles or so, and then we heard a knock on the roof of the cab. We stopped and the Somali reported that the man was now in a critical state. We waited and watched the wounded man slowly die. The Somali knelt down on the road and uttered prayers in the Mohammedan manner. This took the best part of an hour, after which we proceeded to Loliondo with the Somali sitting in front with Sungura and me, Matanda being at the back.

Being inquisitive, I pestered him with questions - how the raid had taken place and how many Masai had taken part. I then asked what sort of arrow had been used, for I knew that the Masai never used them on raids. He put his hand into his coat pocket and pulled out an arrowhead with four barbs, free of poison. I immediately pointed out to him that it was not a Sonjo arrow, which a Tanganyika Masai would use, and therefore it was unlikely that the raiders were from Tanganyika. The only people in that particular area who would use this type of arrow were the Oldorobo, who brought the arrowheads from Kenya. But the Oldorobo did not go in for raiding, so it was most likely that the raiders were from other tribes in Kenya, and had set off in the direction of Tanganyika to confuse their pursuers.

We reported the incident to the District Officer when we reached Loliondo and handed over the body. I heard no more of the matter until six months later when the Somali brought a very young boy to see me. The youth presented me with a big fat sheep for the service I had rendered his dead father, and it was then that I learnt that the culprits were in fact from Kenya, a mixture of Kikuyu and detribalised Masai, and they had been caught near the Mau in Kenya. The ordeal had not upset Matanda or Sungura as it did me, who had never seen a man die before, and they thought it was just one big joke.

At about this time there were a large number of olpuls taking place in the vicinity of our farm, and Matanda kept urging me to go with him on a round of visits to them. I suggested that if he was so keen he should go on his own, but he was unwilling to do this as he would be forced to work for the morans - fetching and carrying for them - unless I went with him. My parents were classified in the category of chiefs; my mother provided the Masai with a considerable amount of medical treatment, being looked upon as a white witchdoctor; and, although accepted as a Masai, I was white after all, and so I was exempted from the unpleasant chores at an olpul and carried both the status of a layoni and that of a moran. Anyone who accompanied me enjoyed the same privileges, especially Matanda who was known as my older brother, and was in fact later named 'The White Boy's Brother'.

After a lot of persuasion I weakened and told Matanda I would go, provided it was not without my parents' consent this time. Eventually, after a great deal of coercion and promises not to leave the Olgosorok forest area, I was allowed out for one night. Needless to say, once we started visiting the olpuls we did not go back after the first night, but a moran who was going home volunteered to report to my family and tell them I would be out for another night.

While on this trip I learnt that the reason for all the olpuls was that the Masai were contemplating a raid on the Sukuma tribe, and were amassing their forces and waiting for the witch-doctor's approval. Unfortunately for them, the District Officer had an excellent information service, and when the Masai eventually held their meeting he arrived too and, instead of the laibon telling them to proceed, he warned them off.

When Matanda and I returned home on the third day I was a bit worried, as I had broken my promise and I expected to be put through the mill. But, to my surprise, when I saw my stepfather, he asked me if I had had a good time and said it was considerate of me to send the moran to let him know I would be late. Provided I did this in future I would get into very much less trouble.

A message had come in my absence from Lexi Trichardt, inviting me to go on a foot safari to Sonjo, where he was to investigate the availability and price of goats for his father. On escapades with Matanda I carried my .256 rifle and Matanda his spear and a Masai sword. He would be dressed in a loin-cloth and I in shirt, shorts and a hat, but no shoes, although we both carried home-made leather sandals that we put on to cross thorny country. But the trip to Sonjo was a completely different proposition. We had a tent, boxes of food, fishing lines, pots and pans, and camp beds. Matanda's remark, when we arrived at the Trichardts' and saw a caravan of no fewer than nine people excluding ourselves, was to the effect that more stuff was being moved than the entire contents of a manyatta.

The first night we spent at Digodigo, camping under some large fig trees next to where the springs came out of the Rift Valley wall. While the camp was being set up, Lexi, Matanda and I went fishing for tilapia, though Matanda did not actively participate in the fishing and was absolutely disgusted when we told him the fish were edible. He refused to have anything to do with them, or even touch them. The Masai do not eat fish under any circumstances. That evening Lexi and I feasted on fish and Matanda disappeared with some others to the Sonjo village nearby.

Later on we heard a lot of singing and dancing so went over to watch. The light was poor, there being only a small fire in the middle of the village clearing, and in the dark very little could be seen. It is at these dances that the Sonjo women choose their husbands. They are a matriarchal people and it is the women who own the property and choose their bridegrooms. Matanda found us in the dark somehow and I asked him what was going on. 'A lot of noise,' was his reply. When I pressed him further he said, 'Who knows what the Olmeg are doing?' This is the name the Masai use for anyone who cultivates land or wears trousers, and is an expression of disrespect. The dancing ceremony was not particularly exciting or interesting, so after watching for a while we went back to our tent.

We went along the Rift wall the next morning and found hundreds of dikdik traps. On our return to camp a friendly Sonjo appeared with some sweet potatoes which he presented to us as a gift. After two days there we moved on to Samunge where the Sonjo craftsmen who made bows and arrows lived. Some of the work they do is as good as most machine-finished articles, and theirs are by far the best-balanced bows and arrows I have seen in any part of East Africa; the Sonjo hunters, however, are not equal to the excellence of their handicraft.

We were going to go on to Sale, but decided against this as Lexi had found out all that was required of him by his father. The Trichardts' cook, Lexi, Matanda and I went straight back to Loliondo, the porters breaking their journey halfway and spending the night at Digodigo. Matanda and I stayed a night at the Trichardts' farm and the following day we went out with Mr Trichardt's brother to shoot a buffalo, as biltong (strips of dried meat dearly loved by the Afrikaner) was running short in the homestead. We passed by several small herds, none of which pleased Mr

Trichardt, but eventually he saw the animal he wanted and waved to us to stand still. We watched him bring his rifle up to his shoulder to fire and heard a slight grunt from the buffalo as it fell. He turned and called to us and we ran up to see that he had shot a fully grown young heifer in beautiful condition. While it was being skinned a group of three Masai appeared from nowhere and stayed to eat the cuts that are permitted by their custom to be eaten while the animal is being chopped up, buffalo being one of the few wild animals they will eat.

Before we left, the Masai asked if they could have the skin for making shields and Mr Trichardt agreed, with the proviso that they did not handle the meat without first washing their hands. Lexi, Matanda and I went back with the ox cart to load the chopped-up carcass and stayed to watch the Masai make their shields.

The skin was split down the centre, making two pieces, and shallow hollows were scooped out of the ground roughly the shape and size of a shield. The rawhide sections were placed in these, outer surfaces down, and the wet skins shaped and filled with river sand. When I asked the Masai whether the hyena would not take the skins at night while they were maturing, they said they would stay there for the four to five days it would take for the shields to mature. They would then take the unfinished shields home and bind them on to wooden frames. Handles would be attached and the shields finally dried and painted with the clan markings, the whole process taking up to two weeks. 'Why don't you take the skins home now and make the shields at your manyatta?' Lexi asked; but the Masai explained that it was much easier for them to bring a goat or sheep to live on for five days than to have the hard task of carrying home a heavy wet hide.

CHAPTER TWENTY TWO

FROM WARRIOR TO ELDER

*I*T WAS OUR CUSTOM, when clearing land in fairly thick bush with scattered large trees, to cut down completely all brushwood that had roots too small to stop or break a plough, and to uproot only the trees and bushes with extensive root systems that were capable of inflicting this damage. The area would then be left for about six months, and just before the heavy rains were expected, a large fire-break would be put in and the section burnt. We usually prepared blocks of twenty-five acres at a time, and once, after burning one of these blocks, we noticed heaps of stones and rocks lying on the surface. We found four of these piles, each with about five tons of stones. As the nearest rock outcrop lay a mile away it was obvious that the stones had been carried there.

We removed the stones from one of the heaps and on digging down discovered a grave. This interested my stepfather and he made some enquiries, but no one seemed to know much. The only concrete clue came from an old man who told us that the area had been used by German soldiers and their African askaris as a refuge during the First World War. We heard nothing more, the matter was forgotten and the land cleared and cultivated.

The following year the adjoining block was cleared. This was found to contain nine more graves; and in a tree, twenty feet up, we discovered the remains of a small platform. When the tree was cut down, the rotting platform disintegrated and from it we collected a human skull and a number of bones. There was also an old army rifle - the barrel rusted up and the wood falling apart - which was later confirmed as being a German weapon of the type used in the 1914 –18 war.

New interest was shown in our finds and John Pride and Otto began to investigate. They learnt that a battle had been fought against the British in the hills two miles away, and the Masai elders, who previously claimed to know nothing about the graves, now gave detailed evidence of the battles which took place in the vicinity of Loliondo, and in particular of what we liked to call 'our' battle.

The main body of the German army moved south over the hills, but a small contingent had been cut off and had positioned themselves on what was now part of our farm. They were surrounded, but held firm and fought until dark, when silence fell. The British, assuming that they had been wiped out, withdrew to pursue a major force of Germans in the south, leaving only a few men to keep watch.

During the night the Germans, not wiped out after all, took advantage of the dark and the reduced British troops, and escaped. They left their dead and two wounded African soldiers to be found by the British the next morning, who buried the dead where they lay.

I was later introduced to the widow of one of the African soldiers. She told me the story of another battle, fought in Narok during the 1920s, in which her son Dangoya had lost an eye and been badly scarred. Major Buxton, District Commissioner at Narok in Kenya, had ordered the Masai to produce morans for road construction work within their districts, so as to enable the Administration to distribute famine relief throughout the area. The elders had agreed to this, but the morans would not co-operate. As Major Buxton would not move to supply the Masai with badly needed food unless they in turn played their part, the elders requested him to help force the morans to carry out this essential work. So, virtually at the point of a bayonet, the morans were rounded up and compelled to work on the roads.

When construction had been completed and the famine relieved, and when there was once again plentiful milk in the district, the morans decided to take revenge on Major Buxton for having insulted them by making them work with their hands. Word went round that the morans were forming for battle, but Buxton did not at first take much notice, until he was informed that the Masai had surrounded Narok Hill with a considerable force.

At the time Buxton had seven police askaris and one European at his disposal, all with rifles. He had asked for help from Nairobi, but no news was heard from that quarter, so with his small party he fought his way through the Masai and got his wife and children away to safety. Then he and his askaris turned back on the Masai and a pitched battle was fought. Although the morans suffered very heavy casualties, they showed no sign of defeat, while Buxton's force was virtually exhausted by the time a company of the King's African Rifles arrived from Nairobi to end the battle.

Buxton had been wounded and the casualties among his men were high. After the dust had settled the leaders of the morans returned and invited the Major to become their leader as, they maintained, he was the bravest of all men. From that day on the Masai regarded him as a hero, showing him the greatest respect, and elders and morans both would do anything for him.

All the moran leaders served a three-year sentence, and among these was Dangoya, who had been shot in the face. Later, when I spoke to Dangoya himself, he confirmed the story as I had heard it from his mother; when I asked him what he thought of Major Buxton, he said that he was the greatest white man ever to come to Masailand, and although many morans had been killed or wounded in the battle, the tribe bore him no grudge.

Which brings me to a point I would like to make about the Masai. They behave very often like overgrown schoolboys, unlike most other tribes going headlong into the fray, knowing or not that they might get hurt; but having done so, they will accept the consequences. There is seldom any weeping after the event, whichever way it goes. If a venture is a success, they are the world's greatest boasters; if a failure, they shoulder the responsibility.

Throughout his entire life the Masai is subject to strict rules and customs which regulate his behaviour, attitudes and social standing, within and without his clan and age-group. To European eyes he appears to lead a hard yet carefree existence, sexually unencumbered and without any apparent morals. But at every stage of his progress: through boyhood, defending his clan and their possessions as a warrior, and finally when he reaches the status of an elder, his life is dictated by the tribal systems and discipline. The ceremony at which a senior moran becomes an elder is called the orgesher or eunoto, and is without a doubt the most secret and most important event of his life – the transition of warrior to becoming an elder (moruo).

The orgeshers take place about once every ten years when the morans are approximately between the ages of thirty-five and forty-five, and the ceremonial sites always remain the same, being chosen for their inaccessibility to outsiders. It was forbidden under pain of death for any other than those participating to attend, but under present-day circumstances many of the rules and standards are changing. Yet it is still very difficult for anyone other than a qualifying Masai to witness an orgesher. I am informed that there are many variations to the ceremony, but the overall rituals performed by the various clans are closely related.

Forty-nine morans, who are also leaders within their groups, are chosen, and of these three outstanding warriors are selected who in turn choose one of their number as their overall leader, the losurutia. The group of forty-nine, and the losurutia in particular, are men who have proved themselves superior to all others in every respect, and the selections are in no way hereditary.

Before the orgesher, forty-eight ordinary huts are built by the women of the area in a circle surrounding a central hut, which is much larger and which must be high enough for the tallest moran attending the ceremony to stand upright without his head touching the roof. In this house, called the osingira, the forty-nine leaders will be initiated.

All other senior morans due for promotion to elders will also participate and will share some of the forty-eight ordinary huts. Complete manyattas too, beyond the confines of the orgesher site, will be built to accommodate the morans. Anyone not having the two extra holes pierced halfway down his ears may become an elder, but may not participate within the central area of the ceremony; their initiation will take place outside the perimeter of the orgesher site. Some initiates who are fully qualified to attend the ceremony in the osingira, however, may choose not to do so as attending the orgesher proper can be expensive for the poorer morans. Beer and cattle for slaughter have to be provided in great quantities for all attending, irrespective of whether they have already become elders or are about to qualify. Also, the losurutia receives five head of cattle from the morans of each area taking part in the ceremony, and he may end up with as many as a hundred animals. This is his due as the appointed leader.

An elder known as the aimesita will brew beer for the losurutia and his group, and this man has to go through a special ritual on the day the orgesher starts. This entails his opening of the gate of his manyatta before daylight and then, as dawn breaks, moving out of his boma, watched by his children who hide behind the huts. He re-enters and approaches one of his oxen which he must kill single-handed by suffocation. The animal is tied down and the aimesita holds its nostrils and mouth closed with his two hands. It may take some time to achieve, but as soon as the beast is dead the orgesher can begin. The aimesita is always one of the previous orgesher's forty-nine, a man chosen for his strength although not necessarily the leader of his time.

Now the morans have their heads shaved, the losurutia first, followed by his two immediate juniors and then the rest of the men. After the shaving the morans will invest themselves with their badges of office which are specially prepared tobacco- or snuff-boxes. No one with an unshaven head may take part (meaning no moran not yet ready to become an elder). At each stage of the ritual the losurutia is the first.

The forty-nine leaders now enter the osingira, and meat from the suffocated ox, cooked by the women, is brought in and served, first on a piece of dried hide to the losurutia by a woman of his choice. She is very important and he must choose a woman who is particularly attractive to him as he will shortly have to prove himself sexually with her in public.

The aimesita now stands up and calls to the losurutia: 'You have proved yourself as a warrior and no shame has ever lain on your shoulders before today, but now, this moment, you have eaten meat which has been seen and touched by a circumcised women, and therefore you have insulted your age-group. Now as a moran you are without dignity. Yet you have good blood, so all that is left to you is to become an elder and sire strong offspring. Therefore you must prove before all eyes that you are still of worth to your people.'

With this announcement, the woman who served the losurutia loosens her skirt, and he forces her out through the door of the hut. The aimesita follows, calling on all to witness the act. Outside, the woman will drop her skirt. At this stage the losurutia should be fully aroused sexually, and he pulls off her upper garment and throws her on to it on the ground. He enters her immediately and the quicker he can reach an orgasm, the more highly thought of he will be. They rise and the woman, to prove that the losurutia has succeeded, will stand with legs apart and the people will see his semen drip down her thighs.

The aimesita will then give the sign that all is well by waving his fly-whisk, and this is also the signal for the start of a general orgy. Women at once undo the waist belts of their skirts, allowing them to drop. They make for the males they fancy, but often are waylaid by other men and, provided they are not of the same clan, copulation is quickly effected. The man will usually push the woman to the ground with his hand which she seizes to pull him down on top of her.

The woman will be with her first partner a bare five minutes before getting to her feet and seeking the next. This initial frenzy gradually wears off, and at the end of the third day the different groups break up camp and the ceremonial site is cleared of any noticeable signs that an orgesher has taken place. The occupants of neighbouring manyattas then become responsible for guarding the secrets of the ceremony and the site until the next orgesher.

CHAPTER TWENTY THREE

THE WELLS AT NGASUMET

*I*N ORDER TO AUGMENT OUR FINANCES, my stepfather used to go out elephant shooting once a year, and although the trophies were not very valuable by today's standards, they usually paid the expenses for a holiday with a little bit over. He was friendly with the Provincial Commissioner - a Mr Murrells, who was stationed at Monduli, the Provincial Headquarters for north and south Masailand - who arranged to take his local leave to go on a shoot with Otto. We travelled down from Loliondo to meet him before going south where big elephant carrying heavy ivory had been reported in the Nabarera, Kibaya, Kijungo and Ngasumet areas.

As this was to be a longish safari and the Administration were putting in a road from Kibaya to Ngasumet, Murrells was able to make it a working holiday. Today, in the dry season, one can leave Loliondo in the morning and arrive at Ngasumet, some 320 miles away, the same evening, but on this trip it took us three days to get to Monduli where we stayed a day, and then a further two days to reach Nabarera where we fixed up a base camp. From there Murrells and Otto went off on foot, leaving my mother and me at the camp.

The men were away five days and returned having shot all the elephant permitted on their game licences. They were very pleased with themselves as the average weight of the tusks was just under eighty pounds, and cause for celebration. As we had plenty of time Murrells suggested that we inspect the new road, which had just been completed. Also, among other things, we wanted to see the famous wells at Ngasumet, which we had heard so much about but had never seen, and although Murrells had described them to us, I just could not imagine their size and depth.

The trip took all day on the very rough new road. On the higher ground the surface was not too bad but in the lower reaches where there was black cotton soil, the elephant, trampling about during the previous wet season, had left large holes which had dried out and become as solid as concrete. As these holes were so numerous only the worst ones had been filled in, and in some places we had to slow down to less than five miles an hour. However, the old Ford chugged along and just before dark we were able to make camp on the high ground near the Ngasumet waterholes.

The area was greatly over-stocked at this time of the year, as there were no other watering points for a considerable distance, and the next day we were awoken by millions of flies which descended on us and never stopped buzzing until night fell. Although I later saw similar wells at other places, the Ngasumet holes were far larger and much deeper; at one, a sloping cutting dug into the ground was over a hundred yards long and about fifteen yards wide at the entrance, descending more than a hundred feet below. At the bottom the cutting narrowed to just wide enough for an animal to move in comfort. At the end of this channel was an enlarged space giving room for approximately ten head of cattle to water at a time. Here a further pit was dug straight down for about twenty feet to the water level; on one side was a small trough made of clay, and here we saw Masai morans doing hard physical labour.

One of the morans went down a crude ladder to the bottom of the pit while another remained at the trough. A rough ox hide bucket, holding about three gallons, was lowered on a rope to the Masai below who filled it, to be drawn up by a third moran who passed it up to the man at the trough to empty. The cattle drank, and as each animal appeared to take in about five gallons the process of watering the whole herd took quite a while. When the first batch of ten had been watered they were driven out and the next lot came down, and so on. The cattle seemed to know the routine, and a moran at the top just banged on a stick when the next batch was due to go down and without any fuss the correct number would break away from the herd and walk down the cutting. As soon as one herd had finished watering, a new herd with its own group of morans would go down the well.

The waterholes belong to individual families, and although they permitted anyone to take drinking water, there was no question of others watering their stock there. The wells were dug by Chagga and other tribesmen such as the Taita, all of whom were originally slaves to the Masai. The very first builders were murdered after they had completed their work so that their secret would die with them, but later well-diggers were kept on for maintenance of the holes and the Masai settled them at a place now known as Arusha Chini. There they were allowed to cultivate the land, on condition that they grew tobacco, which these slave tribes had introduced into Masailand.

Tobacco became very precious and valuable to the Masai, and in order to increase production the slaves were allowed - in fact given - slave women to be their wives and were encouraged to have families. So in time these people of mixed origin became known as the WaArush. However, Masai demands for tobacco grew and the WaArush were unable to increase production because of poor tobacco land at Arusha Chini. The Masai therefore moved them to the very, fertile highland country on the slopes of Mount Meru. This place became known as Arusha and remains so to this day. The WaArush tribe increased in number, taking over almost the entire southern and western slopes of the mountain, and they eventually gained their freedom from the Masai.

Since the original holes were built, others have been dug, and to this day the Masai employ other tribes to work for them to maintain the wells. The labour entailed is quite considerable, as invariably during the rains large landslides occur, filling in the entrances and making the tracks dangerous to both humans and cattle, and often partly clogging the waterholes themselves. Each year they have to be cleaned out and sometimes deepened as the water level seems to be getting lower.

At one time poachers and the Oldorobo would use the welts for trapping and killing game at night, making it impossible for cattle to water the following day, particularly when big animals like elephant had died along the channels. So the Masai tried to put a stop to this by putting up brushwood surrounds, but when these were broken down by thirsty elephant they had to allow such animals to drink, instead placing moran guards to keep the poachers away.

It was our intention to stay at Ngasumet for a few days, but the flies drove us away and we decided to move on to Kibaya through Nabarera, Murrells still enjoying what he called his working holiday and attending to official matters in these outposts of his province. The rains broke just before we reached Nabarera, and the black cotton areas, so common in these parts, had to be circumnavigated. This involved clearing new tracks and filling in holes, but I had a very enjoyable time. We had two days in Monduli while Otto took the lorry into Arusha for repairs, then we set off for home. We were cheerful about our successful safari and in good spirits, but on our arrival in Loliondo we were greeted with the bad news of an outbreak of rinderpest which had reached our herd.

There was a period at Loliondo when the surrounding Masai manyattas were continuously losing cattle from some unknown disease, and in those days the Masai did not consider the Veterinary Department to be of any use, seeing them rather as a hindrance to the free movement of stock - and certainly no good at curing sick animals. That was at about the time when the first preventative treatment for rinderpest was discovered but not perfected. Consequently in certain cases the losses from the injection itself were quite numerous and the Masai were very opposed to their cattle being treated.

It was unfortunate that, while cattle were dying of rinderpest and from the inoculation, there was also an outbreak of anthrax. This made the Masai yet more adamant, as any animal that had been treated for rinderpest and subsequently died, they claimed had been killed by the injection. The veterinary authorities were also having difficulties trying to stop the Masai from eating dead animals, as they would not believe that anthrax was so widespread in the area, nor would they accept the fact that an anthrax-infected carcass was dangerous to humans.

Matanda, some other boys and I were out hunting one day and, watching a Masai herd go past, we noticed that one animal had been left behind, dead. It was in good condition and seemed to have collapsed and died for no apparent reason. One of the boys ran after the moran who was herding the cattle while the others and I looked about for the snake we were so sure must have bitten the ox. Just then a car approached on the road which was not far off and I waved for it to stop. It was the Veterinary Officer with some of his guards. When I told him what we had found, he inspected the beast and did not take long to diagnose anthrax. In order to confirm this, he ordered the guards to open the carcass, and by the time the operation had been completed the owners of the herd had arrived on the scene.

They were told the animal was not to be eaten under any circumstances, as the disease that had killed it was also injurious, and possibly fatal, to man. This the Masai pooh-poohed and they told the Veterinary Officer they would not touch the meat only if he paid for it - otherwise it was their property to do with as they liked. The Veterinary Officer was very busy at the time with his rinderpest inoculation campaign and could not spare anyone to keep guard over the dead ox so he left it, again warning the Masai of the likely outcome should they eat the meat.

No sooner had he driven away than they skinned the animal and immediately began to eat those parts which are usually eaten raw. In the end nothing of the ox was left - every piece was either eaten raw or taken away to the manyatta. Matanda had his share too. I do know for a fact that nobody from that manyatta died within the year, or complained of any sickness which could resemble anthrax; yet slides had been taken by the Veterinary Officer and anthrax was confirmed. However, on another occasion a long time after this, a group of Sonjo tribesmen ate a sheep thought to have been killed by anthrax, and two of them died.

I had eventually persuaded Matanda and the others that we should go home, looking at them anxiously from time to time and quite certain they would drop down dead. These thoughts, however, were soon cleared from my mind when we came across a colony of mongooses all standing up in a circle in the middle of the road. Fortunately our dogs had been taken off by the Veterinary Officer in his car as he did not trust us to keep them from feeding on the infected carcass, so we were able to approach the mongooses quite close without their paying us any attention.

They had surrounded a five-foot-long puff-adder, and in the

centre a small mongoose was fighting the snake alone, the others standing around them on their hind legs, squeaking and chirruping at one another and every now and again looking to see if we were keeping our distance. The lone mongoose would approach the snake and entice it to strike; as the snake did so, the mongoose would jump away and then back at the snake, digging its teeth into the puff-adder's neck. This was repeated continuously for over an hour, the snake's reactions becoming slower and slower until finally it lay dead. The little mongoose very tiredly dragged it towards the long grass beside the road and the rest of the colony followed, all of them disappearing in a matter of minutes.

I had noticed that, by the end, the puff-adder's neck was bloody and completely stripped of skin; and the fascinating aspect of the battle had been the speed of the mongoose's movements, sometimes getting to within an inch of the snake's head before it could retaliate. The other point of note was that not one of the other mongooses made any attempt to help.

CHAPTER TWENTY FOUR

THE OLDOROBO

*M*ATANDA'S FAMILY HAD ANOTHER STROKE of bad luck when one of the older sons was badly mauled by a leopard. Remembering how well Matanda had fared under my mother's care, they brought him too to our house for treatment. I had nothing whatsoever to do with his eventual recovery, but some time after he had returned home to his manyatta, Matanda told me his brother wished to give me an ox to bind our friendship. I was very bucked about this and told Matanda I would like to be a friend to his brother, but that it would be difficult as he was a moran and I was not.

'Don't worry about that,' Matanda answered, 'he will be our olpiron when we are circumcised.' We both thought this would be a very good idea.

As the brother's manyatta was some fifteen miles away, I persuaded my parents to let me have one of our Nandi herders to go with me to collect the ox. Although we started out very early, Matanda, the herder and I arrived at the manyatta in the late evening, for we had spent much of the day chasing game. We were met by Matanda's brother and taken to his junior wife's hut where we were fed. Soon after eating, Matanda and his brother got up to go, the brother saying to his wife, 'Treat my guest as my olpiron.'

The Nandi herder and I had just climbed into the big bed when the young wife turned to me and said, 'You can come to my bed if you wish.'

I made excuses why I should not, and the Nandi suggested that he should go to her bed instead. This she refused, saying that I was the guest of the house and if I did not sleep with her, no one would. The Nandi pointed out that the white man or boy was not allowed to go to any woman's bed unless she was his wife. 'And what's more,' he went on, 'Debbe is only a layoni. Do you know that white men do not marry until they are old men?'

She thought this was a great joke and made no bones about it, saying, 'What good is any man to a healthy woman when he is already an elder?' She also said she thought white girls must be very unhappy as they could have no real pleasure from old men who were not their true loves.

The Nandi tried once again to be allowed into her bed, but she was adamant, saying that if he did not show her the respect she was due, she would complain to the elders. This ended the discussion and we all went to sleep.

Early in the morning Matanda's brother let me choose my ox from eight he had picked out from his herd, and I felt so proud of my new possession I could hardly wait to get home to show everybody.

The Trichardts had packed up and abandoned their farm, as they too had experienced hard years and Mr Trichardt said that he could not afford to plant another crop and risk losing it, although the rains were due and prospects for a good season looked promising. He had not the money to plough and prepare his land, and as it turned out his was a wise decision.

As a result of their moving out, a settlement of Oldorobo had sprung up on the Trichardt farm, within a couple of hundred yards of the old farmhouse, in caves at the bottom of a deep gorge. Matanda and I met one of our Oldorobo friends in the forest and he invited us to come and see how they prepared poison for their arrows.

This preparation consisted of taking bark from new shoots of the mrisho tree, which looks very much like an olive tree. The finger-thick roots were also used and pounded together with the bark to a fine pulp. This was then put into a large earthenware pot with water to the brim and boiled continuously for three days and nights. As the water evaporated away, more was added until the expert poison-maker announced that it was ready for drying.

At this stage the liquid was strained off and boiled separately. No more water was added and in due course, when the necessary evaporation had taken place, a gooey, black, tar-like mixture was left. This was tested by dropping a bit on to a hot coal: if it sizzled with tiny bubbles it was deemed successful; if it boiled up into one big bubble it was thrown away. If successful, the poison could now be put on the arrows, and when cool would set hard. During the whole of this process no woman was allowed anywhere near the camp, for if a woman were to see the poison in the making, it would be flabby and not stick to the arrows, and when used would not penetrate the skin of a shot animal.

The Oldorobo camp appeared to be for the purpose of renovating their equipment and, in conjunction with the poison-making, there was a great deal of activity on repairs to bows, making new arrows and bowstrings, and honing knives. This was the only time I have ever seen the Oldorobo in what might be termed a camp. When I asked why they had chosen this particular spot they said that from time immemorial their group of the Oldorobo had come here to work, but when Trichardt had been given the farm they had been forced to find a less satisfactory site.

The Oldorobo is not, as many people believe, an offshoot of the Bushman or the pygmy, but is a direct offshoot of the Masai. He is somewhat shorter than the Masai and less refined in appearance, owing to Bantu blood introduced by slave wives purchased from the Masai who had taken the women from other tribes. They are rather unkempt-looking, as to them a man is not in any way to be judged by his appearance, but by his ability as a hunter. They are usually extremely brave, but have a complex regarding their inferiority to the Masai.

The Oldorobo are generally known by Europeans as the honey hunters. They live on game, berries, roots and honey; and pay no taxes. They sleep on the ground, on large rocks, or in trees; and their groups, which usually consist of from ten to forty individuals, inhabit the forests and game areas throughout East Africa. The Masai version are the true Oldorobo, although there are offshoots from other tribes who live in exactly the same manner but speak different languages. One of these, the Watindiga, is the second largest Oldorobo-type group in Tanzania.

The Oldorobo proper, the Masai claim, are descendants of the Loitayo clan who, during a famine years gone by when they lost all their cattle, were forced to take to the forests and plains to live on game in order to survive. After the drought a majority of the clan assembled and formed an army of warriors who raided other clans to replenish their herds. However, a small proportion preferred the life of the forest and remained there. These were the forebears of the Oldorobo groups, of which there are now a number throughout Masailand. Because there used to be a great deal of intermarriage amongst them, the proportion of deformities is high. Although the Masai consider them to be inferior, they do consult them on a number of matters.

One day, when I was in the forest to the south-east of Loliondo, I shot a huge eland but we were too far from home to carry it back.

A friend of Matanda's who was with us mentioned that there was an Oldorobo party not very far from where we were - indeed they were probably lurking in the bushes nearby at that moment - and he offered to go and call them. He was soon back with an elderly Oldorobo. He was the first true Oldorobo I had ever seen, and after accepting that we had no intention of doing him or his friends any harm, he made a sign to what appeared to be the trees and suddenly, from nowhere, seven other Oldorobo emerged. I gave them the eland but told them we would come back for the skin if they would dry it for me.

I became friendly with this particular group and got to know them well. From time to time I would take them salt and matches, and, in return they gave me various herbs, arrows, bowstrings and arrow poison. I learnt from them that they occasionally worked for the Masai, circumcising the youths, plaiting morans' hair and supplying honey for making beer. They also worked at olpuls, carrying water and collecting herbs for the various soups. In the highlands around Ngorongoro and Kilimanjaro, they split cedar into planks for making Masai bomas, which they also helped to build.

The Oldorobo are without a doubt the best hunters in East Africa, and are very strict about respecting one another's hunting grounds. Sometimes a detribalised Oldorobo may find himself working for a white hunter as a tracker, and if he is good the European is more or less certain to acquire a reputation in the world of big-game hunting, for the Oldorobo tracker has an uncanny ability to find game of the type required. However, a lot of so-called Oldorobo trackers are no more Oldorobo than I am.

CHAPTER TWENTY FIVE

FAREWELL TO LOLIONDO

*T*HE RAINS HAD STARTED AND IT WAS TIME TO PLANT, so for the next five weeks most of my days were spent helping my stepfather on the farm. Our fields this year were in tiptop condition and the planting was a great success. All was now looking very good, and there were rumours that the price of maize would be increased. The big job of cultivating between the maize rows was on, and labour from Sonjo was plentiful, particularly as we were asked to employ as many tax defaulters as possible. So far as we were concerned, these were the best labourers, as the prison warders were there to see that they carried out their tasks without any argument. They were given rations and six shillings a month, three shillings of which was taken for tax.

One evening, while the new District Officer, who had taken over from John Pride, was having a drink with us, he remarked on how well the crop was looking. Otto said, 'Yes, it does look good. And thank God - for if we have another failure we will be finished.'

But, at about three-thirty one afternoon shortly after, Matanda pointed to the north: 'Look at that dust cloud over there!'

I looked and asked him what it could be.

'Don't you know?' he shouted. 'It's locusts!'

I immediately ran to tell Otto, who sounded the fire warning gong. When the labour force had congregated some were ordered to bring tin cans and others to start fires along the edges of the fields. When the locusts arrived, the place looked and sounded like a battleground with the smoke and banging tins, but nothing we could do would stop them settling on the young green maize for the night. The next morning the fields were bare but for little stunted maize shoots, and the forest behind us looked as though an aircraft had sprayed it with silver paint - all the young shoots had been stripped of their bark. It was a disaster.

My stepfather was terribly depressed, but the Kikuyu labourers on the farm tried to encourage him, saying that provided the locusts did not return, all the small maize - which was nine-tenths of the crop - would survive and yield well, and that no further cultivation would be necessary as the locusts had eaten off all the weed too.

A week later the maize was showing signs of recovery, and in no time at all it was looking good again. The locusts did not return and the Kikuyu had been right. But just when the maize was about to cob we had a very heavy hailstorm, and the crop was completely destroyed.

The outcome of this second calamity was that we were finished. We had already lost more than half our livestock through rinderpest, we had no money and no banks from which to borrow. There were not even sufficient funds to feed ourselves or the labourers.

Otto took the difficult decision to sell off the remaining stock and any movable machinery, and to reduce the labour force to the barest minimum. My mother and I were to stay on the farm for the time being to sell what we could while he went back to the Lupa. As soon as we had completed the sales and paid off all our men, or alternatively, if Otto was able to send enough money to do this, we were to pack up and join him. We were virtually destitute. My mother was left with just enough cash to keep us in flour and sugar for the next six months and that was all. For the rest we had to fend for ourselves and hope to recover something from what we could sell.

I was fourteen and had become quite an effective young bushman, so the obvious thing for me to do was to trap our food. This I did, and I was able to keep the house supplied with meat - mainly yellow-neck francolin, guinea-fowl, spurfowl and a range of other birds from small finches to pigeons, and dikdik, impala and wild pig. Shooting was out, as we had no money to buy ammunition. Sometimes my Masai friends would give me some meat to take home from an ox they had slaughtered.

This situation lasted about eight months, but before we heard from Otto the position became more and more desperate. Although on the whole our labour force behaved very well, some of our newer employees began to play on the fact that they had not received their wages and instead of being a help were more of a headache to my mother, who was finding it very difficult to cope. By the time the long-awaited letter did arrive, she was at breaking point. Otto had sent enough money, but only just enough, to pay off our men and for our fares to the Lupa.

Matanda and I had become so attached to each other that, although I was looking forward to the move as children always look forward to something new, I dreaded the day of parting. I discussed this with my mother who was very sympathetic and helpful to both Matanda and me, and pointed out that we would be parted for just a short time during which Matanda would probably be circumcised and have to go to live in a moran manyatta, while I would have to go to school. Then we would meet again.

Shortly after the talk with my mother Matanda approached his father on the subject of his circumcision and was told he would be going off with one of the first batches and should therefore attend the forthcoming ngipataa, which is where he was on the day we left. As Matanda could neither read nor write and I could barely do so, letters were out of the question.

It was now well into the rainy season and the road from Loliondo to Arusha over Ngorongoro was impassable. The rains would continue for quite some time, which would mean either staying on at Loliondo for at least another two months and using up our fare money, or going the long way round through Nairobi. However, Mr Ker Singh came to the fore and offered to take us up to Nairobi where we could stay with his family for a couple of nights.

I was extremely embarrassed in Nairobi, as I was used to wearing no shoes. I was given a pair and told to wear them at all times. The Indian boys I was to play with thought I was a most peculiar sort of European; firstly for not being able to wear shoes and walk in them properly, and secondly because I was so backward and not interested in their civilised lives and activities.

Although the Ker Singhs were very kind and hospitable, our stay in Nairobi was not a happy one, as we had no money to spend or to repay them for their goodness to us, and we were only too pleased to board the train for southern Tanganyika.

Christmas was drawing near and we hoped to get to the Lupa in time for it. Otto had meanwhile arranged for me to go to the new school in Arusha in mid-January and my mother wanted a bit of time to get me outfitted. This was a bitter disappointment to me, as I had convinced myself that school was neither necessary nor desirable, but I saw that there was no avoiding it, as both Otto and my mother were adamant that I should have some education. So, it was off to boarding school I went. My days as a barefoot white Masai were over.

CHAPTER TWENTY SIX

EPILOGUE

*I*N THE YEAR 1952, I was a free-lance Cattle Dealer with a contract to purchase all Tanganyika Packers' slaughter stock for the Arusha Cold Storage Plant. Special markets had been scheduled for Northern Masailand, one of which was to be at Loliondo.

For some time I had been looking forward to the day when I would be going back to this area, in the hopes of meeting up with my boyhood friend. Being a nomad, he could be anywhere, and by Masai custom, names of people changed at just about every ceremony they went through. I decided to send ahead one of my Masai drovers and his gang, to try and make contact with my old friend, and if possible advise him of my coming.

On account of the state of the road, due to rain on the Ngorongoro Crater, I arrived at Wasso (7 miles from Loliondo) where the market was to be held, late at night. There were a lot of cattle and people around, but no-one I recognised, and as it was late, I decided to go to a waterhole I knew of from old times to set up camp. I arrived to find that a Government Rest-house had already been established there, but since it was empty and obviously not in use at the time, I set up camp. I made use of the Rest-house, but sleeping in my vehicle because the Cash Box containing over £50,000 was bolted to it.

The armed drovers were stationed around the camp. Such precautions were advisable since Mau Mau insurgents from Kenya, just over the border, had been reported active in the area; so far, only against their own people. There were a number of Kikuyu and half-Kikuyu tribesmen living in and around Loliondo.

That night, I thought about my old friend, wondering whether or not he had been located. However, the next morning I did not have to wait for long, for I had just finished shaving when Matanda himself appeared suddenly at the door of the Rest-house, his hand outstretched in greeting and saying "Enkakuyaa Ngasa". (Enkakuyaa - brother).

We were both jubilant at seeing one another after all the years, but after the initial exchanges, quite suddenly, I found myself at a loss for words. I had to stop Matanda and try and explain rather clumsily that I had hardly spoken Masai for the last eighteen years, and then only very slowly, so we would either have to talk in KiSwahili, or through an interpreter. Matanda's KiSwahili was definitely worse than my Masai, and he was not keen on speaking through a third party, so this was the first setback to our renewed relationship.

The next came when I declined to go with him to his Manyatta, where he was all set to kill an ox in celebration. I could not safely leave the cash unattended, besides which, I had to attend the market over the next two days.

"Does this mean that you will be sleeping here in the bush even though I, your brother, have offered you the hospitality of any one of my three wives' houses?" he demanded.

I tried hard to explain that I could not abandon my work since this was my means of livelihood, and Tanganyika Packers were anticipating a lot of cattle from this particular Market. Hence, if I failed to produce them, I stood to loose my Contract and would be labelled unreliable.

Matanda, however, could not be persuaded.

"But, you are not buying cattle at night!" he argued.

"No. But I still have to look after the cash and work on the books for the day's buy, besides which my staff expect me to be here with them," I replied.

"I will send moran to look after your Ngosholla (money) and the camp," he said.

I replied, "If your cattle were in an area on the move, where there were known to be fierce lions, and I asked you to leave them to the care of other people in order to come and spend the night talking to me, would you do so?"

He said immediately, "But, cattle are not money. Now you talk just like the other Olmeg, comparing cattle with money!"

Time was getting on, and I had to leave for the Market, so I presented my old friend with a heavy tartan rug, an ex-army Greatcoat, plus some beads for his womenfolk. This pacified him temporarily, particularly as I told him not to kill that ox until I had returned from the sale.

I did not see him again for a couple of hours or so until suddenly I heard my Masai name, "Debe!" I looked round and there was Matanda pointing to two head of cattle, which he said were his, adding that a third was behind in the next batch, and that he expected me to buy the lot for a good price. I did, and as soon as he had collected the money for the last animal, he departed and did not turn up again until the next morning. I was beginning to think that he might have taken offence, but that evening when I got back to camp, I found a fat sheep tethered outside the Resthouse and was told that it had been sent by Matanda for me to eat.

Because Matanda was not there to share in the feast, I did not slaughter the sheep that night. The next morning he turned up and immediately demanded, "Why have you not eaten the sheep I sent for you?"

I explained to him that I did not want to eat it without him being present, and since it was difficult for me to come to him on this occasion, why did he not instead come to my camp and stay with me for the night. I added that, the next time, I would stay with him. His answer was that he would not come for the night, since he had to bring in more cattle the next day, but that he would come and eat meat with me that evening, and would bring one of his children who was in need of eye treatment.

The Market closed at five in order to give the traders a chance to sort out their purchases and we had to leave the following day by 2 p.m.

Having searched for, and found, two missing animals, which had strayed into one of the Somali herds, I eventually got into camp, feeling both exhausted and thirsty, at about ten minutes to seven. My friend was already there with his latest wife; a very comely young girl of about 20 years of age, and with her were her two children - a girl of between 2 and 3 and a boy of about 9 months strapped to her back. Both children were suffering from eye trouble, so I treated them, after which the wife and her brood were sent off home. Matanda, a couple of his friends and me, settled down to a drink of beer, although it was strictly speaking illegal for me to give them any alcoholic drink. Matanda had slaughtered the sheep, most of which was already roasting on the fire.

We spoke long of the old times, pausing briefly now and then to cut off and eat pieces of meat and take a sip of beer. Occasionally, Matanda would call over one of my servants and hand him a well-cooked morsel.

This went on until about 10 p.m., by which time the meat was coming to an end. Eventually, Matanda announced that he was going home, and that since the Market would be finished the next day, my staff and I was expected to spend the night at his Manyatta. I tried to explain to him that I had to go on to the Olalaa Market, but would definitely be back again soon, and would then be able to stay with him at his Manyatta.

He left abruptly, turning on his heels without even a Goodbye. Nor did he turn up the next day with his cattle for sale, but sent them instead with someone else. Two years were to pass before I saw Matanda again.

Then one day, I flew into Loliondo to investigate the likelihood of moving cattle from there to the Leibig's factory at Athi River in Kenya. The usual hordes of people gathered to look at the plane, and among them was Matanda.

He greeted me in a very friendly and warm manner, saying, "So, you have kept your promise. You have come back to see me!"

In fact, I had not intended staying the night, but I hadn't the heart to say this. Instead, I found myself saying, "Yes, of course."

Having completed my business with the District Officer at Loliondo, I returned to the plane and invited Matanda to come up with me for a brief flight, since I had to inform the Nairobi Control that I would not, in fact, be returning to base until the following morning.

Matanda quite obviously enjoyed the flight and became very excited when I flew him low over his own Manyatta. When we landed, he produced two morans to guard the aeroplane, and we set off to his Manyatta, which was a couple of miles distant. Having got there, I was taken to the hut of one of his wives and was told that I would be occupying it, while Alexander, a cattle buyer who had accompanied me, was about to be taken to another. Hurriedly I told

Matanda that it would be quite in order for us two to share the same hut. He shrugged and instructed his wife to make some tea telling her that I did not drink milk; something he must have remembered from our childhood days. He then went off to get a goat slaughtered and cooked outside the Manyatta. This would later be served on wooden skewers.

A little later he was back with some young elders, all of whom wanted to be taken up for a flight in the aeroplane. I would have been happy to oblige had I not been short on fuel, but there was just enough to get me back home, with about half an hour's reserve in case of bad weather. I was in the process of trying to explain this to Matanda and his friends when a car turned up with a Catholic Priest, who had come to ask if I could help out by flying a very sick sister to Arusha. This, I agreed to do the next morning. It would be a quick flight, and I would be able to take on more fuel at Arusha having dropped off the patient. This was explained to Matanda, and we eventually set off together, along with two of his friends.

When I landed again, there must have been a hundred or more people waiting to be taken up for a flight. No amount of explaining could convince them that I simply could not take them all, so eventually I locked up the plane and walked away towards the Manyatta. I had gone at least 300 yards before Matanda and a couple of others condescended to follow me.

As we approached the Manyatta, we could see the cattle heading back for the night in the distance. Inside the Manyatta, I was escorted to another hut, and here about eight of us sat down. A calabash with a bubble neck was produced. Matanda took a sip and passed it on to me. It contained over a gallon of honey beer, tasting very akin to strong mead and with pieces of comb and the odd dead bee floating about. I took a sip, spitting out the roughage, and duly passed it on to the next person, but by this time, a second calabash was doing the rounds; then a third and a fourth! Meanwhile, the circle began to increase, as did the smoke and acrid smell of sweat in the hut, but the beer and goat meat was excellent and the company very interesting. Matanda never stopped recounting tales of our boyhood escapades and the others kept on butting in, while outside the women could be heard singing to the cows whilst milking.

Eventually, the woman of the house announced to her man that the beer had come to an end. Matanda apologised profusely to me, saying that, had he known that I was coming, all his wives would have been put to making beer. I assured him that I had had more than enough.

"Then, my brother, let us go and talk in amongst the cattle," he said. The women had by this time finished their milking and the young girls were rounding up the calves and putting them inside the huts, whilst the elders barricaded the Main Gates. In the distance we could hear the Moran announcing their approach. The slight breeze was heavy with the smell of cow dung and olive smoke from the burning fires inside the huts, as Matanda and I strolled casually amongst the cattle exchanging views on a variety of subjects, ranging from Politics, the Mau Mau, our boyhood days together, personalities known to us both, and suchlike. Every now and then he would pause beside a particular animal and relate something of interest about it. We spoke in a mixture of Masai and KiSwahili for well over an hour, and once again I found myself becoming immersed in Manyatta life. Finally, he led me back to the hut in which I was to sleep and where Alexander was already installed. The blanket I always carried with me was laid out and Matanda informed his wife that I was both his best friend and his brother, and that she was to look after me well during the night. He then swung on his heels and left, whilst his wife turned to me saying that her hut was mine to use as I wished.

The hut was very hot and smoky, but the young woman seemed to sleep well, getting up a couple of times to add more sticks to the fire. By contrast, Alexander and I not only found the heat oppressive, but also were constantly disturbed by bedbugs and the scuttling of cockroaches – so much so that by the morning, I had come to the conclusion that Masai life would no longer suit me. However, when I got up to relieve myself amongst the cattle, and heard the women singing gently as they milked, an atmosphere of calm tranquillity and contentedness triggered the old relaxed feeling I remembered so well. I found myself thinking that we so-called civilised peoples missed a great deal by allowing our lives to become so complex that we were alienated from true Nature. On the other hand, it would be virtually impossible to shrug off the responsibilities that attend civilisation, and drop out into a way of life far removed for so long. My thoughts were suddenly thwarted by the arrival of the Sister whom I was to fly to Arusha, but on the return flight, I once more pondered such matters. Although the gap between Matanda's thinking and mine on certain

subjects had been largely bridged by an understanding that enabled us once again to become great friends, there was undoubtedly something intangible now missing in our relationship, due no doubt to the very different upbringing we had had during those intervening years. Whilst he had not changed much, I had. A chance remark made by Matanda after I had landed brought this home to me.

"So, you now fly this machine in the air, and I can't. We are different," he said.

I asked him if he would like to be able to fly, to which he replied, "You go on flying your machine, and I will go on looking after my cattle," adding as an afterthought, "But we must see and talk to one another every now and then, since we are both now becoming old."

And, we will.

CHAPTER TWENTY SEVEN

MY SEARCH FOR MATANDA

48 YEARS LATER...

Sixty eight years on from those days of playing barefoot in the Serengeti, and 48 years after last seeing Matanda, a chance meeting urged David to try to find his friend once more. These are his words...

*H*AD I REMEMBERED MATANDA'S FAMILY NAME, the search would have been a lot easier, but with this vital information missing, and with changes of physical locations, age-group names, and inter-clan marriages etc. over the years these elements combined to make it an impossible task and I was forced to abandon my quest. However, the desire did not die, and some 68 years on, from those days of playing barefoot in the Serengeti, and 48 years after last seeing him, a chance meeting urged me once more to try to find my friend.

At the Braeburn school fair in Arusha during the year 2001, I was displaying my books for sale on the Meat King stand. A woman approached Lesley, who was helping out on the stand, and remarked that she was the grandchild of Dangoya, the Masai warrior who features in my historical novel 'Waters of the Sanjan.' She wanted to buy one of the books. The author (Lesley pointed me out) would sign it for her. The woman came over and spoke to me briefly, but as there were a lot of people gathered around, all asking questions about the books, we swapped addresses and agreed to make contact later. I was excited to find out that Dangoya's family were still about and this gave me a clue, and the idea that I should approach the search for Matanda through them.

I contacted the woman, made plans, and on a set day in 2002 I went off to Loliondo. Dr. Moll and his wife from the Wasso hospital had invited me to visit and would give me all the help they could.

I had not been to Loliondo for over 45 years and with the exception of very much reduced game all along the route; the physical area was much the same as I remembered. However, the changes in customs that had taken place, particularly the agricultural cultivation before and in Wasso, were obvious all the way to Loliondo. There were hardly any Masai dressed in Masai traditional dress, and I only saw Masai manyattas that had both corrugated iron and thatched roofed huts. Loliondo was a mass of concrete and corrugated iron and very little sewage control. Wasso had a semblance of Masai occupation, some people were in Masai dress and both Masai and Swahili were spoken and there were a few cattle about. On the cattle market days, Masai culture was much to the fore, on account of most of them coming in from outside to trade their livestock.

On arrival I met up with Dr. Moll, who very kindly took me around the hospital and introduced me to two of the Dangoya family. Enquiries started straight away with a trainee nurse named Linda Dangoya, who informed me that she had taken the next day off and would act as a guide.

On the 4th of May 2002 I set off with Linda Dangoya and Adam my driver to try to find my old friend who may or may not still be alive and who I had neither seen nor heard of since 1954. We first went to see Mr. Peter Kasha, who had been the first Masai Loliondo D.C. at independence in 1961. After explaining the situation, Peter said that this was going to be difficult but he would come with us and see what could be done. We called in at the original trading post and found my friends old corrugated iron house and shop, built in 1930 –

still standing but abandoned. We then moved down to where our farmhouse was built in 1932; there was nothing left and the area had been cultivated. I was saddened by the disappearance of the olgoss orok forest and the whole of the forested hillside next to our old house. Linda's mother's home as situated very close to the spot where the 'puss moth' had landed in front of our house in 1932-33, which had at the time been a clear strip, and was still there. This landing as mentioned in my book 'Barefoot over the Serengeti'. Joyce Ndangoya – Linda's mother gave us tea, biscuits, cashew nuts, groundnuts, and after a lengthy discussion took us to a Masai manyatta where we spoke to some elders, both male and female, without much success, but they mentioned the name of an old lady at Loliondo, who Peter knew.

Also one of them had heard of 'Debbe' associated with a white lioni of a long time ago. (Debbe was my Masai name). We then went back to the car, but first had to go back to Joyce's house, where I was presented with a beaded fly switch, an elder's talking stick (normally used by chiefs) and three fine beaded bracelets. We then called on the old lady in Loliondo. Peter went ahead and having first spoken to her we were invited into her room, which was very dark. She could only just be seen lying on her bed, but could not be recognized. She must have been very old or ill, but appeared to be clear witted. No one else but Peter and me were allowed in the hut. She did not appear to be able to speak in anything but Masai. She had heard of 'Debbe' a long time ago, but could not connect it with anybody. She knew and remembered Dangoya, so I asked her if we could go through some names of the daretoi age group. She said it was a long time ago, but could remember some and started to name them. She mentioned the name Olemunga. I immediately stopped her, for this name long-forgotten, suddenly leaped back into my memory. Matanda's family name had been Munga! I asked her what she knew about Olemunga (which means son of Munga). She told us that he was a very rich man and had been a chief of the Loitayo clan both in Kenya and Tanganyika, but had died a long time ago. Peter recognized the name and said he had known him. The old woman then said. 'Why don't you go and ask Halango Munga who lives just up on the hill, she is the daughter-in-law of Kaiti.'

Peter knew the place. I was getting excited as I had a feeling that we were getting somewhere. Halfway up the hill to Halango's house the road got very bad. We had to leave the car and walk about 500 yards. Peter was immediately recognized and greeted with affection. I was introduced and we were invited into the home which was built of concrete blocks, corrugated iron roof and consisted of two rooms and a kitchen. The first room had a settee, and two arm chairs with a low table, a cupboard, and a small high table with two straight backed chairs, and two windows with curtains. She wore an ordinary dress and her daughter Aipano was dressed likewise. After the normal greetings were over Peter asked her if she knew whether her husband's father (Kaiti) had a white friend when he was a young boy. She replied that she had heard of a young lashomba lioni (white boy) called 'Debbe' who went everywhere with Kaiti, and whose mother gave Kaiti medication after he had been badly mauled by a leopard and saved Kaiti's life. She then asked Peter if I knew of that lioni. Peter replied 'Why don't you ask him?' She turned to me and asked if I knew this Debbe - I replied 'Yes'.

'Is he still alive?'

I said 'Yes'.

'Where can I see him? Is he far?'

Peter then said 'Look at him well'. He is standing in front of you'.

She turned to me and said 'You!'

I said 'Yes'. Whereupon she put her arms around me and started to cry. Her daughter Aipano did the same from the other side. I felt very embarrassed, but cheered at the same time. We all broke away from one another – the old girl went into the bedroom and came back with a very nice beaded talking stick and a kanga which she presented to me, saying. 'That is the talking stick that Kaiti used and I want you to have it as you are our father now.' The kanga is for the first born daughter'.

It transpired that Matanda was actually renamed Kaiti following his circumcision and passage into warrior hood. His full name, therefore, and for many, many years had been Kaiti Olemanga. No wonder no-one had remembered the name Matanda!

Meanwhile Aipano brought out fresh and sour milk and was making tea. I declined the milk, but partook in the Masai tea and biscuits. Halango, Peter and I started questioning and discussing. Halango wanted to know how many wives, I have and how many are still living. I said 'One and she is not very well now'.

'And children?'

'I have one daughter, three nieces and one nephew and they all have lots of children'.

'Why did you not bring any of them to look after you?'

'I did not know that I was going to find you and they live a long, long way away, but I shall try and bring them as soon as they come to visit me.'

I then asked questions. Through a series of interrogations, I established that Kaiti later became an elder, was made chief of the whole Loitayo clan, both in Kenya and Tanganyika. He had 4 wives, who bore him children. Halango had been married to David, one of

Kaiti's sons. I was driven almost to tears when I heard Matanda had named three of his sons after my family (David after me, Norman, after my brother, and Otto after my stepfather!) who died some time ago, and she had five children living – two boys and three girls. Aipano never married, but had three children and she – Aipano – became a teacher at the Loliondo School and lived with her mother. Kaiti apparently died (reason unknown) in 1956, just two years after I had last seen him. When I last met him in 1954 he was already an important chief, but had said nothing to me about it. He also had the three sons at that time, such was his humility.

So, I had found Matanda, even though posthumously. The search was over. Sadness and elation mixed as salty tears on my cheeks, and none could be told apart.

The time came for me to leave, as it was getting late. Both Halango and Aipano tried to make me stay longer, saying I was their only father they had left. They made me promise to come back with my family. I do not know if I ever will. I am now eighty, and do not travel as well as I did. Time will tell, I guess, as always.

April 2003

From left: Halango Munga (Kaiti's daughter in law, wife of David Ole Munka - one of Kaiti's sons), the author David Read and Aipano.

Other books by
David Read

Beating about the Bush
(the sequel to Barefoot over the Serengeti)

Waters of the Sanjan
(a historical novel of the Maasai)

Copies of these books are available from:
www.serengetimasai.com
davidread@serengetimasai.com

CROSSING THE SIABEI